COLLINS GEM

BIKE BOOK

The Diagram Group

D1097368

HarperCollins*Publishers*

Information given about road safety in Chapter 3, 'The Cyclist', is intended only as a basic guide to cycling on the road. It is not comprehensive and is not intended as a substitute for manuals about cycling safely on the road or for the *Highway Code*, both of which cyclists are strongly advised to consult.

HarperCollins Publishers
PO Box, Glasgow G4 0NB

A Diagram book first created by Diagram Visual Information Limited of 195 Kentish Town Road, London NW5 8SY

First published 1994

Reprint 10 9 8 7 6 5 4 3 2 1 0

© Diagram Visual Information Limited 1994

ISBN 0 00 470538 6

Printed in Great Britain by
HarperCollins Manufacturing, Glasgow

Introduction

Collins Gem Bike covers all the main aspects of
bicycles and cycling in eight fully illustrated chapters.

The bicycle deals with the basics: what a bicycle is,
how you propel and balance it, what each part does and
consists of and how you can maintain and repair your
machine.

Bicycle field guide begins by telling you what to look
for in choosing and buying a bicycle. The main kinds
of bike you will encounter – and some unusual ones
you might not – are also described.

The cyclist covers the human aspect: from learning to
ride to signalling, riding in traffic, coping with special
situations and avoiding accidents.

Cycling for fitness shows how graded training on bikes
– outdoors and in – strengthens muscles and boosts
heart–lung performance: the key to fitness.

Touring gives tips on bikes, equipment, route-planning
and touring techniques.

Racing looks briefly at all main types of competitive
cycling, including bikes, gear and racing techniques.

Cycling for fun explores mountain-bike users' off-road
riding techniques.

Perfecting the bicycle lists landmarks in the bike's
evolution, and spotlights modern advances in human-
powered vehicles from the mountain bike, monocoque
frame and recumbent road bike, to pedalled boats and
aeroplanes.

Contents

1. THE BICYCLE

2. BICYCLE FIELD GUIDE

3. THE CYCLIST

4. CYCLING FOR FITNESS

5. TOURING

6. RACING

7. CYCLING FOR FUN

8. PERFECTING THE BICYCLE

1. The bicycle

WHY BIKES MATTER

Bicycles are marvellous machines for many reasons.

Efficiency Bikes are arguably the most efficient method of transport, superb at converting muscle power into rolling motion. Cycling uses only about one-fifth of the energy of walking, and you can travel far faster and further by bike than on foot.

Low cost You can buy a reliable bike for a fraction of the price of a car or even a motorbike. The only fuel it needs is the food you eat. You can learn to maintain and repair your bike cheaply at home.

Durability Cars last about 10 years. If you replace parts as they wear out, a bike might last you a life-time.

Compactness Slipping through city traffic by bike can be quicker than driving. In town, you can park a bike almost anywhere. At home, you can store it in a small shed. Several bikes will fit on a car's boot rack or roof rack. Bikes are so small and light that many ships and aeroplanes will carry them free.

Universality There are bicycles, tandems or tricycles to suit people of almost all ages and cycling abilities. **1** We show the percentages of different types of machine used in the UK in 1990.

Usefulness Cycling to work is a healthy alternative for people working within about 11km (7mi) of home. You can also make useful, short shopping trips on a bike which is equipped with a basket or panniers.

Pleasure Cyclists see, hear and smell more of the

countryside than drivers shut up in cars. A cyclist can stop to look at a view without first having to find somewhere to park. Mountain bikes can explore places cars cannot reach.

Health Regular cycling improves fitness and can help to prolong life.

Environmental friendliness Bikes do not pollute the air with fumes and noise as cars do, and they need much less road space than cars.

1 Bicycle types used in the UK

a Mountain bicycles 38%
b Children's bicycles and tricycles 17%
c Action bicycles (BMX, etc.) 17%
d Racing bicycles 8%
e City bicycles 7%
f Shoppers 7%
g Sports/touring bicycles 6%

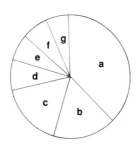

HOW BIKES WORK

A bike moves (**1**) as you push pedals (**a**) around with
your feet. From the pedals, rods called cranks (**b**) turn
an axle (**c**) which turns a toothed chainring (**d**) that
turns an endless chain (**e**). The chain turns a small
toothed wheel called a sprocket (**f**) on the back wheel,
which revolves the wheel's hub (**g**). Spokes (**h**) fixed to
the hub turn the wheel's rim (**i**) and air-filled rubber
tyre (**j**). The spokes act as levers, like legs (**2**) sticking
out from the hub. Each spoke (**a**) ends at a point on the
rim and tyre, which behaves much like a foot (**b**). The
whole rim and tyre work like a circular row of feet
placed heel to toe. At any one time, one spoke and its

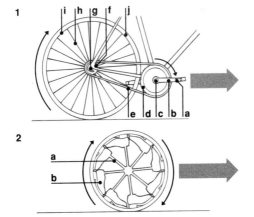

'foot' push back against the ground to thrust the bike forward. As each 'foot' lifts off the ground, the one in front takes its place.

Balance You can stand upright (3) because your body is balanced against the downward tug of gravity: a vertical line from your centre of gravity (**a**) falls inside your base (**b**), your feet. A stationary bicycle topples because it is unbalanced. A vertical line through its centre of gravity (**c**) tends to fall outside its narrow base (**d**), its wheels. A skilled rider can balance on a stationary bike by leaning it from side to side, as you can balance one end of a long stick on your finger. Keeping a moving bike upright is easier. A spinning wheel is more stable than a stationary one. To negotiate a corner (4), the rider must lean his or her bike at an angle. The rider's speed and the 'tightness' of the corner determine how much he or she will have to lean into the bend. The greater the speed, the more the rider has to lean.

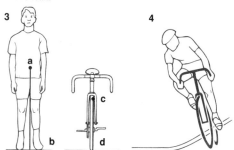

ANATOMY OF A BICYCLE

A bicycle (**1**) is a bit like a human body (**2**). Support is
provided by tubes (**a**) instead of bones (**b**); a bicycle
has cables (**c**) instead of nerves (**d**); and wheels (**e**)
instead of legs (**f**). Its muscles are yours.

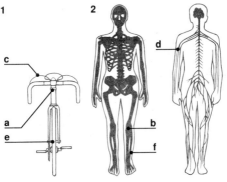

3 A bicycle has up to 3000 parts, including tiny items
such as ball bearings. Here we list the main parts you
can see. The frame (**a**) supports the rest of the bike, and
the rider. Its fork (**b**) supports the front wheel; its seat
stays (**c**) and chainstays (**d**) support the rear wheel.
Handlebars (**e**) turn the front wheel and support the
rider's arms, brake levers and maybe gear levers. The
saddle (**f**) supports the rider's body. The seat post or
seat pin (**g**) supports the saddle. The front wheel (**h**)
features tyre, spokes, rim and hub. The rear wheel (**i**)

includes tyre, rim, spokes, hub and sprocket – or several sprockets of different sizes which together are called a freewheel block. Pedalling turns the rear wheel via a transmission system (**j**) involving pedals, cranks, chainring, chain and sprockets. Gears (**k**) include gear levers, cables, and either an enclosed hub mechanism or an exposed derailleur mechanism with a set of sprockets. Gears vary the distance a pedal moves to turn the back wheel once. Brakes (**l**) include brake levers, cables and arms applying the brake blocks to the wheel rim.

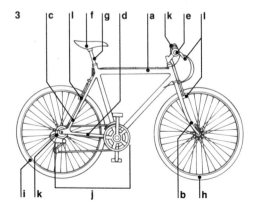

THE FRAME

The frame (**1**) is the skeleton supporting the rest of the
bicycle. It combines strength with lightness, being
made of hollow tubes welded, brazed or glued together
to form a top tube (**a**), head tube (**b**), down tube (**c**),
bottom bracket shell (**d**), seat tube (**e**), seat stays (**f**) and
chainstays (**g**) with drop-outs (**h**). The fork (**i**) forms an
item separate from the rest of the frame (see p.20).
Frame tubes can be metal (steel, alloy steel, titanium or
aluminium), or made of composites, notably carbon
fibre. Stickers on alloy-steel tubes show make and
grade (e.g. Reynolds 531; Columbus Aelle). The best

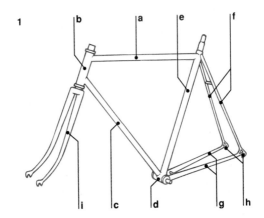

materials are light and strong, yet resilient and flexible
enough to absorb shocks. A tube wall (**2**) can be (**a**)
plain gauge (of uniform thickness), (**b**) single-butted
(thick at one end) or (**c**) double-butted (thick at both
ends). Butting reduces weight without sacrificing
strength.

Frames come in various designs. They include diamond
(**3**), European open (**4**), mixte (**5**), American open (**6**),
and camelback (**7**). Women's bikes traditionally have
open or mixte frames, but many women prefer diamond
frames, because their design is the strongest.

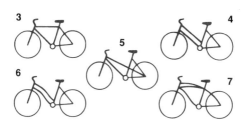

HANDLEBARS

Handlebars (**1**) support your arms and steer the bike by turning the fork (**a**), which holds the front wheel. The bars themselves (**b**) are of steel, alloy or carbon fibre, covered by a soft grip, sleeve or tape (**c**). The bars (**2**) are attached to a handlebar stem (**a**) by one or more binder bolts (**b**). To tilt the bar ends on dropped handlebars up or down, loosen the binder bolt(s). If the handlebars rotate around the stem, tighten the bolt(s). In a typical bicycle, the stem's lower end (**3**) sits in the fork tube (p. 20), and the stem and fork tube fit inside the frame's head tube. An expander bolt (**a**) runs down

1

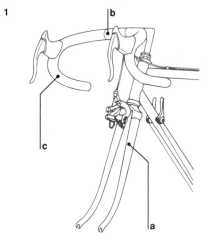

through the stem, holding a wedge nut (**b**) in the stem's split lower end, forcing that out against the fork tube to lock the stem firmly in place (**c**). To raise or lower the handlebars, loosen the expander bolt, adjust bar height and retighten. Once loosened, the expander bolt may need a light downwards tap with a hammer before the handlebars can be raised or lowered. Be sure to leave at least 6cm (2in) of stem inside the head tube. Tightening the expander bolt may also cure any side-to-side play on the handlebars.

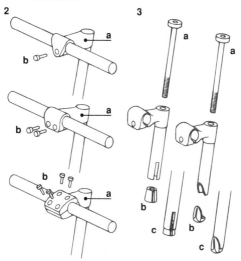

TYPES OF HANDLEBARS

Here we show some of the main types of handlebars.

1 Mountain-bike handlebars are flat and straight. They should be wide to give good control when riding off-road. Narrower ones can be used when riding on the road.

2 Flat 'bucket-handle' handlebars are mainly seen on sit-up-and-beg roadsters.

3 Profile bars give a 'cowhorn' effect. They provide good upper-body support and access to brake and gear levers, but produce an inefficient sit-up-and-beg riding position unless used on bikes with a short head tube.

4 Dropped handlebars come in three forms: Maes (a) with a level top bar and shallow drops, Randonneur (b) with a top bar upswept at both ends, and Pista (c) with a downcurved top bar and deep drops. The first is for general use, the second for touring and the third for racing. Dropped handlebars support the upper body, reduce spine-jarring shocks, cut wind resistance and aid comfort by allowing changes in riding position. The four riding positions (**5**) are with hands: (**a**) on the hooks (for riding fast or into wind), (**b**) on the brake levers (in traffic), (**c**) on the brakeheads and (**d**) on the top bar (in quiet conditions).

6 Clip-on aero-bars with adjustable armrests give a low-profile riding position. They reduce drag, shaving seconds or minutes off the time a racing cyclist takes to complete a time trial or triathlon. But they make braking difficult.

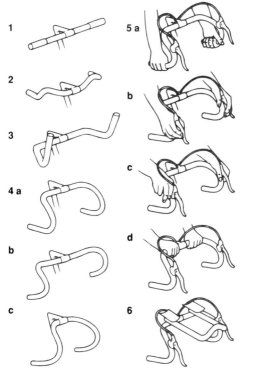

1

2

3

4 a

b

c

5 a

b

c

d

6

FORK AND HEADSET

The fork (1) supports the front wheel and is turned by
the handlebars. It comprises a fork tube (a) and fork
blades (b) with drop-outs (c) into which the front-wheel
axle slots. The lower ends of the fork blades are raked:
they curve forward, more so in a tourer than in a racing
bike. A raked fork makes a bicycle easy to steer.

The fork tube is pushed up inside the frame's head tube
and joined to the head tube by a two-part headset (2),
which features two sets of ballbearings that help the
fork to turn freely and without undue wear. The top part
of the headset includes a locknut (a), a bearing cup (b)
screwed into the fork tube, and ball bearings (c) in a
cup called a ball race (d), which is screwed into the
head tube (e). The lower part of the headset at the fork
crown includes a bearing cup (f) screwed into the head
tube, and a second set of ball bearings (g) in a base
bearing cup (h) on the fork tube.

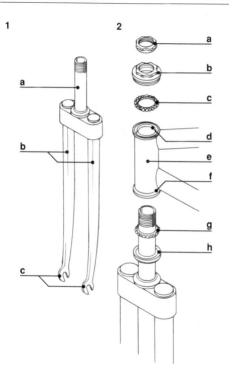

1

a

b

c

2

a

b

c

d

e

f

g

h

SADDLES

When you sit on a bicycle, much of your weight is
conveyed through your pelvic bones (**1**). Women have a
broader pelvis than men, so a woman's saddle (**a**) needs
to be wider than a man's saddle (**b**). Saddles come in
various materials and weights, and with different kinds
of suspension. They include narrow lightweight racing
saddles (**2**); nylon-based anatomic saddles (**3**) padded
to support the pelvic bones; springy, gel-filled saddles
(**4**) for greater comfort; and coil-sprung saddles for
rides over bumpy tracks (**5**). Bouncing on sprung
saddles wastes pedalling energy; unsprung leather
saddles are reputedly best for long-distance work, but
some need breaking in and all need protecting from
rain. Commuting and touring cyclists of both sexes tend

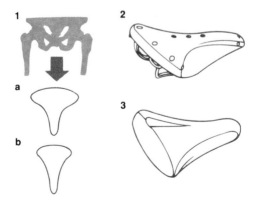

to prefer a broader saddle than the kind made for men's racing bikes. Choosing the right saddle can make the difference between comfort and agony, but you will only find out which suits you best by sitting upon it mile after mile. A gel-filled saddle cover can be a fairly cheap solution for any discomfort.

You might need to adjust your saddle's position and angle (**6**). To raise or lower the saddle, loosen the seat-post binder bolt or quick-release lever (**a**), leaving at least 6.5cm (2in) of seat post in the seat tube. To slide the saddle forward or back, or to tilt its nose up or down, loosen the nuts or micro-adjust the seat bolt under the saddle (**b**).

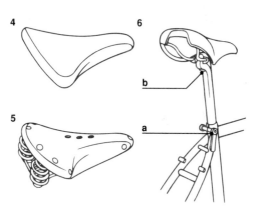

SUSPENSION SYSTEMS

In the 1980s, designers began adding suspension systems to mountain bikes to lessen the jolting suffered by cyclists who ride fast down rough mountain tracks. Besides increasing comfort, a suspension system improves the tyres' grip. The results are improved handling, and faster climbing and cornering, lopping about 2 minutes off what on a rigid-frame bike is a 10-minute, high-speed descent.

Suspension systems compress on impact to absorb a bump, then rebound ready for another. There are two main types of system: elastomer and spring/oil.

1 Elastomer systems These have springy rubber components that shorten to damp down or absorb shocks. A hard elastomer (**a**) bulges (**b**) as it shortens. A microcellular elastomer (**c**) contains air holes and shortens without bulging (**d**).

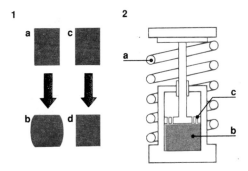

2 Spring/oil systems These combine a coil spring (or pressurized air) (**a**) with damping by oil (**b**) valved through tiny holes (**c**).

Suspension systems can be built into various parts of a bike. Arguably, front fork suspension (**3**) is the most essential; front and rear suspension can be better still. One all-round system (**4**) has suspension built into the handlebar stem (**a**), and a swing-arm seat-stay/chain-stay unit (**b**) joined to the seat tube by an elastomer bushing (**c**).

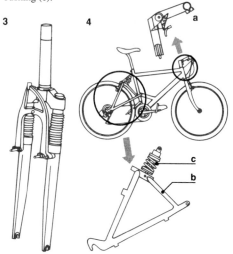

TYRES, VALVES AND PUMPS

Tyres have an outer casing protecting an air-filled inner tube, usually with a Schrader valve (**1**) or Presta valve (**2**). Each needs a different pump. Unscrew the nut at the Presta valve tip before pumping and screw it up afterwards. Pumping up a tyre fills the inner tube with springy compressed air which cushions your ride. There are two types of tyres: wired-on and tubular. Most bikes have wired-on tyres (**3**). These comprise an inner tube (**a**) in a casing with reinforced edges (**b**) to hold the tube onto what is usually a high-pressure (HP) wheel rim (**c**). Wired-on tyres tend to wear well, retain air well, and resist punctures. Racing bikes have narrow tubular tyres (**4**). These comprise an inner tube (**a**)

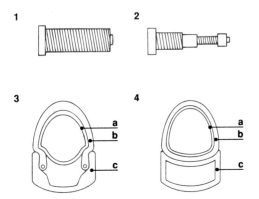

sewn-up inside an outer cover (**b**) glued on to a tubular rim (**c**). Tubular tyres give a faster ride than wired-ons, and the whole tyre is quicker to replace, but tubulars puncture more readily and are harder to repair.

Some types of tyres grip better or go faster than others. Racing cyclists prefer a tyre that is smooth, narrow and highly inflated (**5**). For off-road riding a broad, knobbly, underinflated tyre (**6**) gives the best grip. An intermediate type of tyre (**7**) 32cm (1¹/₄in) wide, with some tread, and kept fully inflated, suits everyday road use.

To prevent splash-up from the tyres in rain, most bikes have alloy, plastic or stainless-steel mudguards.

5   **6**   **7**

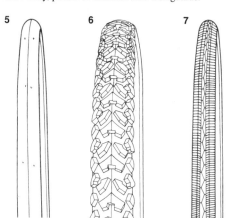

PREVENTING AND MENDING A PUNCTURE

To prevent punctures, keep tyres fully inflated, inspect
for wear or stones in the tread and beware of broken
glass in the road. But go prepared with a pump, spare
inner tube, and repair outfit, containing tyre levers,
patches, and rubber cement. Metal tyre levers are only
suitable for steel rims. Plastic levers can be used on
both steel and alloy rims. To mend a punctured wired-
on tyre, unscrew the valve locknut and push the valve
up through the rim (**1**). Being careful not to pinch the
inner tube, lift part of the tyre cover over the rim by
slipping tyre levers under the edge of the cover and
hooking them onto the spokes (**2**). Finish this task by
sliding your finger along inside the cover. Lift out the
tube, pump it up and find the puncture by turning the
tube against your face until you feel air escaping (**3**). If
you feel none, a leaky valve might be the trouble; dab
the valve with saliva to see if this bubbles. If both
methods fail, see if bubbles appear from the tube when
you dip it in water. When you find a puncture, mark it
with a pencil or a piece of chalk (**4**), then dry the tube
and sandpaper an area around the hole a bit bigger than
a repair patch. Thinly spread this area with rubber
cement. When it has dried, peel the foil from a patch
and stick this over the hole, working out from the
centre (**5**). Squeeze the patch hard onto the inner tube.
When the edges of the patch are well stuck down, peel
off the plastic or paper backing very carefully. Ideally,
use powdered chalk or talcum powder to dust over the
glued area to prevent sticking. It doesn't hurt to do this
all round the inside of the tyre. Partly inflate the tube to

prevent creasing, and ease it back inside the cover onto the rim, with the valve in its hole (be aware of possible directional tread) (**6**). With both hands, work the cover onto the rim (**7**); the last bit is the hardest and you may need to use tyre levers, though excessive use of these may stretch the tyre. Lastly blow up the tube.

If out on a ride, it is quickest to replace the faulty tube with a spare and repair it at home.

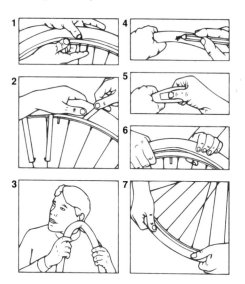

RIMS AND SPOKES

Bicycle wheels must be strong but light, for the heavier
a spinning wheel, the greater its inertia and so the
greater the steering and stopping effort required.
Bicycle makers claim that paring a gram off the wheel
is worth a kilogram off the frame. They build wheels of
lightweight alloy rims and narrow, stainless steel or
plated or galvanized spokes. Rims can be (**1**) tubular,
for use with the tubular tyres used in sprint-racing
bikes, or (**2**) HP (high-pressure) for use with wired-on
tyres, used on most other bikes. Spokes come in various
lengths and gauges (thicknesses). They can be plain-
gauge (**3**) (of uniform thickness) or double-butted (**4**)
(thicker at both ends) for extra strength. Each spoke has
a head (**a**), a blade (**b**) and a threaded end (**c**). The
threaded end is pulled through a hole in a flange on the
wheel hub – a hole too small to let the head through. A
nipple (**d**) inside the wheel rim is then screwed down
through a hole in the rim onto the threaded end until the
spoke is held taut. Rims for racing bikes have holes for
28 or 32 spokes; touring-and-mountain bike rims tend
to have 36; tandems and heavily-laden touring bikes
have 40.

1   **2**

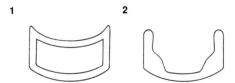

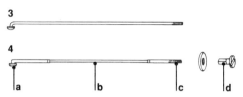

Alternate holes in the rim support spokes from alternate sides of the hub. Spokes from one side can be laced over and under each other to produce different spoking patterns: two-cross (**5**); three-cross (**6**), suitable for racing; or four-cross (**7**), suitable for touring and everyday use.

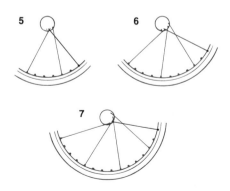

TRUING A WHEEL

A collapsed wheel can be a disaster, but you can
prevent it by checking your bike for warning signs,
especially one or more loose or broken spokes, which
throw the wheel out of true so that it wobbles.
1 Test spoke tension by plucking. All spokes should
feel and sound firm. Those on the rear wheel's
freewheel side should be slightly tighter than those on
the other side. If any spoke seems too tight or too loose,
remove the tyre and adjust the spoke (**2**) by turning a
spoke key (**a**) applied to the spoke's nipple (**b**).

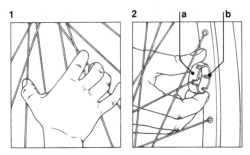

To check for lateral distortion (**3**), spin a wheel while
holding a piece of chalk against the front fork or a seat
stay, so it almost touches the side of the rim (**4**). Long
chalk marks on the rim show where spokes most need
adjusting. One quarter turn at a time, tighten those
spokes which go to the side of the hub opposite the
chalk mark.

To check for radial distortion (**5**), spin a wheel with chalk fixed over the top of the rim (**6**). At the chalk-marked high spots tighten all spokes.

After adjusting spokes file down any that jut up from the rim and might cause a puncture.

To replace a broken spoke, remove the tyre, unscrew the spoke nipple with a screwdriver and push the spoke out of its hole in the hub flange (**7**). Reverse this procedure to install a new spoke, lacing it in the same way as the rest.

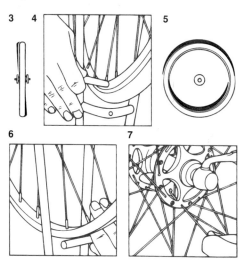

HUBS AND THE FREEWHEEL MECHANISM

The hub of a bicycle wheel (**1**) is an assembly of items including: spindle (**a**), hub casing (**b**), ball bearings (**c**) and cones (**d**). The wheel rotates around the spindle (axle), which slots into the front or rear drop-outs, and is held in place at each end by a locknut (**e**) and wheel nut (**f**) or quick-release lever. The hub casing revolves around the spindle on two sets of ball bearings, each in a cup held in position by an adjustable cone. Each end of the hub casing forms a flange (**g**) pierced with holes for the spokes. Two cone spanners (**2**), one applied to a locknut and one to a cone, can help you to tighten or

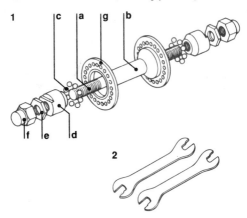

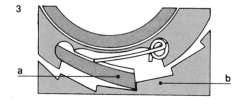

loosen adjustable cones and dismantle the hub to grease or replace worn bearings. Sealed-bearing hubs need less frequent attention.

One end of the rear wheel's hub casing supports a toothed wheel, or sprocket, turned by the chain to turn the rear wheel. Derailleur gears (p.46) have several sprockets. Each sprocket surrounds the freewheel body, attached to the hub. When you freewheel, tiny levers called pawls click past the sloped teeth of a ratchet wheel inside the freewheel body (**3**). When you pedal, each pawl (**a**) locks into a tooth (**b**), and the ratchet transmits your power to the wheel. There are freewheel remover tools (**4, 5**) and sprocket remover tools (**6**), but some are specialized. For most cyclists, fitting new sprockets or freewheel bodies are tasks best left to an experienced bicycle mechanic.

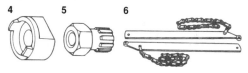

BRAKES

Most bicycle brakes are worked by levers mounted on
the handlebars, which pull cables that force rubber or
compound brake blocks against the wheel rims. Springs
pull the brake blocks off the rims when the levers are
released. The left lever acts on the rear wheel, the right
on the front wheel. Here we show five types of brake.

1 Side-pull brakes These are controlled by a cable (**a**)
with side attachment to two curved arms (**b**) bearing
brake shoes (**c**) and pivoting on a central bolt (**d**). Good
side-pulls act fast and are light to control.

2 Centre-pull brakes These have a centrally-mounted
cable (**a**) pulling on a short connecting cable (**b**) acting
on two arms (**c**), each with a pivot bolt (**d**). Centre-pulls
have a light action and great stopping power, and need
infrequent adjustment.

3 Cantilever brakes These have a central cable (**a**)
pulling on a long connecting cable (**b**) leading to arms

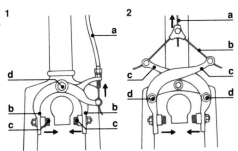

(c) pivoting on mountings (d) brazed to the seat stays and fork. Cantilever brakes give an even more powerful performance than centre-pulls or side-pulls. Most mountain bikes have them.

3

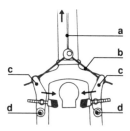

4 Hydraulic brakes These work like car brakes – with a piston compressing fluid in a cylinder. They are easy to operate, immensely forceful and more effective than most brakes in mud or rain.

5 Motorcycle-type disc brakes These also have great stopping power, but need a heavy hub mounting.

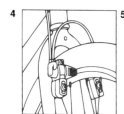

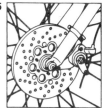

BRAKE MAINTENANCE

Replace brake blocks before they get badly worn. Make
sure you get the right type for your brake system and
rims (steel or alloy). To replace a worn traditional
rubber brake block, use a spanner to remove its metal
brake shoe from its arm (**1**). (Many modern brake
blocks have integral attachment bolts and do not sit in a
separate shoe.) Using pliers or a screwdriver, prize the
block from its shoe and gently hammer in its
replacement (**2**). Replace the brake shoe, making sure
that the open end faces back and both blocks align with
their rims.

1

2

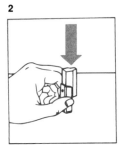

To replace a frayed side-pull brake cable, use a spanner
to undo the brake-lever nut (**3**). To adjust the brake
after replacing cable or brake blocks, use a friend or
third hand (a special tool) to hold both brake arms
together against the rim (**4**), while using pliers to pull
the cable through before you tighten the fixing nut. You
can now fine-tune by turning the barrel adjuster (**5**) to
move the brake blocks slightly in or out.

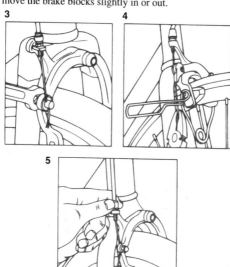

PEDALS

A pedal should provide a firm nonslip support for the ball of your foot in its shoe. The three main types of pedals are platform, cage and system.

Platform pedals provide broad flat surfaces as supports. Rubber platform pedals (1) have rubber inserts for use with ordinary shoes. They are fitted to children's bicycles and heavier adult bikes such as roadsters. Metal platform pedals (2) are for use with cycling shoes. These pedals are each likely to come with a toe-clip and strap (3), which increases your pedalling power. There may be a ridge to take a cleated shoe – a special cycling shoe with a plate that projects from the sole. Platform pedals are suitable for touring and everyday use.

Cage, or rat-trap, pedals (4) include alloy pedals with narrow, serrated surfaces for good grip. Some can damage shoes with soft rubber soles. When using the quill pedal shown, the outside of the foot rests against a projection (a) (the quill). This racing pedal comes with toe-clips and straps. Parallel cage pedals (5) lack a quill, so you can use them either way up. Many mountain bikes have them.

System pedals (6) are lightweights designed for compatible cleats to lock into so securely there is no need for toe-clips or straps, and releasing your feet is easy. Some take recessed cleats in cycling shoes that double as walking shoes. You can get system pedals and shoes for mountain, racing and touring bicycles.

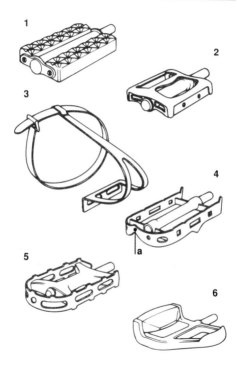

1

2

3

4

a

5

6

PEDALS, CRANKS AND BOTTOM BRACKETS

A pedal is attached to one end of an arm called a crank. The crank's other end is attached to the chainring/s and the spindle (axle) rotating on bearings in the bicycle frame's bottom bracket. Cranks transmit pedalling motion to the chainring/s.

A pedal (**1**) includes a body (**a**) rotating on bearings (**b**) around a spindle (axle) (**c**) supported at its outer end by a cone (**d**), with a washer (**e**), a locknut (**f**) and a dust cap (**g**). The pedal spindle's inner end is screwed into a hole at the small end of a crank. The crank's big end is attached to a spindle inside the bottom bracket shell. A cotterless crank (**2**) is attached by bolts (**a**), and a cottered crank (**3**) by a cotter pin (**a**). There are also one-piece units comprised of cranks and spindle. You need different tools for removing different types of crank.

A conventional bottom bracket assembly (**4**) comprises spindle (**a**), ball bearings (**b**), fixed cup (**c**), adjustable cup (**d**), lockring (**e**), washers (**f**) and bolts or nuts (depending on axle type) (**g**). Such systems require periodic checking and greasing, but now you can get cartridge bottom brackets which are easy-to-fit and maintenance-free. Sealed construction protects their bearings from wear caused by dirt.

Replace bent pedals or cranks. Grinding or clicks as you pedal might mean a loose crank, pedal or bottom bracket spindle requiring adjustment or worn parts needing replacement. The cranks and chainring/s are often referred to as the chainset.

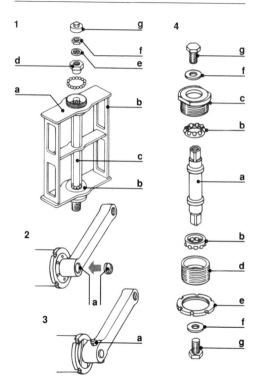

CHAINS

Bicycle chains come in several widths and qualities.
Each chain is an endless series of roller bearings: a loop
made of about 166 links which mesh with teeth on a
chainring and a sprocket. A well-maintained chain
transmits 98 per cent of the chainring's motion.
Clunking or a slipping chain could mean a warped
chainring or worn teeth on chainring or sprockets. As
with most of the moving parts in a bike, a chain
receives heavy use. It needs regular cleaning (p. 54)
and checking for wear. To check for wear, try lifting the
chain off the big chainring (**1**). If you can see a whole
tooth, replace the chain and maybe the sprockets with
new ones (seek advice if you are not sure).
To replace a derailleur chain you must break one of its
links. A derailleur chain's links (**2**) comprise alternating
pairs of inner (**a**) and outer (**b**) link plates with bushings
(**c**) secured by rivets (**d**).

1

2

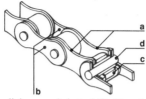

To break a link, use a chain tool (**3**). Place the chain in the tool with its pin (**a**) opposite the end of one rivet (**b**). Turn the tool handle to push the rivet out of the holes in its links. If you intend reusing the chain after cleaning, leave one end of the rivet in an outer link plate and bend the chain at the link until the chain ends separate. To reassemble the chain, use the chain tool to push the rivet back through the holes in the other three links. Your chain tool should come with instructions about the number of turns each operation requires.

3

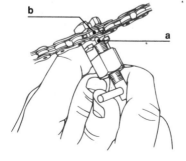

DERAILLEUR GEARS

A bicycle's gear system transmits the motion of your feet from pedals to back wheel. The simplest bikes have one gear. On a bike with several gears, the one you are in decides how far the wheels travel each time the pedals turn once. In a high gear, one pedal turn takes you further than in a low gear, but for more effort. Low gears make hill-climbing easier. By changing gear as you ride up and down hills you can keep an efficient cadence (pedalling rate). For most people this is 65–85 revolutions per minute.

There are hub gears (pp. 52–3) and derailleur gears. Derailleurs offer the most gears (up to 21 or more) and the widest spread (pp. 48–9).

Derailleur gears derail the chain from one toothed wheel to another. Many gears are worked by (**1**) two thumb shifters (**a**) or rotary shifters (**b**) on the handlebars or two gear levers (**c**) on the handlebars or down tube. (Indexed gears give the cleanest shifts.) To change gear you should ease off but keep turning the pedals. Operating the controls activates the derailing mechanisms (**2**). The right-hand control tightens or slackens a cable moving the rear changer (**a**) in or out to shift the chain between toothed wheels called sprockets (**b**) on the outer part of the rear wheel's freewheel body. A jockey roller (**c**) and tension roller (**d**) are sprung to keep the chain taut. Operating the left-hand control tightens or slackens a cable, shifting the front changer (**e**) in or out to nudge the chain from one chainring (**f**) to another.

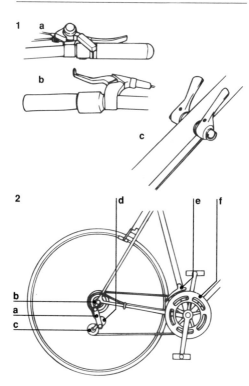

GEAR NUMBERS AND SIZES

In a derailleur gear system, the number of gears
depends on the number of sprockets and chainrings
with different sizes and numbers of teeth. Two
chainrings and five sprockets give 10 gears. Three
chainrings and seven sprockets give 21 gears. The
highest gear is the one with the chain on the largest
chainring and smallest sprocket (**1**). The lowest gear is
that with the chain on the smallest chainring and largest
sprocket (**2**). If the largest chainring has 52 teeth and
the smallest sprocket has 13 (a ratio of 4:1), turning the
cranks once turns the bicycle wheel four times. If the
smallest chainring and largest sprocket each has 28
teeth (a 1:1 ratio), turning the cranks once turns the
bicycle wheel once. Two chainrings with 50 and 40
teeth and five sprockets with from 28 to 14 teeth would
give a wide spread of gears.

Gear sizes are expressed in inches, as chainring teeth
divided by sprocket teeth multiplied by wheel diameter.
This dates from the pre-multigear days of penny-
farthing bicycles when each turn of the pedals turned a
wheel once, and gear size depended on wheel size. A
good spread of gears can make a 68cm (27in) wheel
equivalent to a 229cm (90in) wheel (**3**) for tailwinds, a
101cm (40in) wheel (**4**) uphill and a 71cm (28in) wheel
(**5**) for very steep climbs.

Derailleurs are extremely popular. However, their
exposed mechanism can need fairly frequent
adjustment and cleaning.

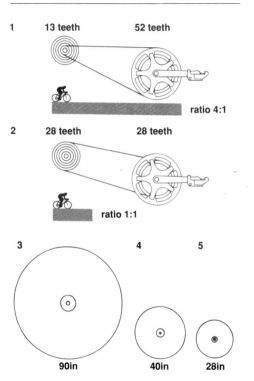

1 13 teeth   52 teeth

ratio 4:1

2 28 teeth   28 teeth

ratio 1:1

3

90in

4

40in

5

28in

DERAILLEUR ADJUSTMENTS

Sometimes a chain slips off the inner or outer sprocket
or will not hop onto one or the other. To reseat a slipped
chain, push the jockey roller forward (**1**) to slacken the
chain so that you can lift it back onto its sprocket. On
the rear derailleur (**2**), there are two small adjustment
screws (**a**) labelled L (low) and H (high). If your chain
came off between the inner (lowest gear) sprocket and
spokes, set the chain on the inner sprocket and smallest
chainring. Turn the L screw a quarter clockwise to
move the rear changer outward a little. If the chain
came off outside the outer sprocket, turn the H screw
slightly clockwise to move the rear changer inward a
little. If, in either case, a quarter turn does not work,
keep adjusting (in the right direction) a small amount at
a time, until correct. Remember that the chain can
break the spokes if it comes off inside the sprockets.

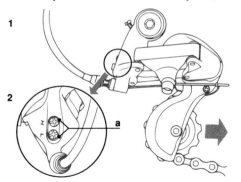

The front derailleur (**3**) has its own adjustment screws
(**a**): H for the large chainring, L for the small chainring,
which move the cage (**b**), guiding the chain slightly in
or out.

To test screw settings, change through the gears while
cranking the pedals by hand with the rear wheel
supported off the ground.

Test for slackness in the gear cable by putting the chain
on the smallest sprocket and lifting the rear derailleur
cable with a finger half way along the down tube. If the
cable is slack, loosen the cable fixing bolt and use
pliers to pull through surplus cable (**4**) before tightening
the bolt again. (Locations and types of cable fixing
bolts vary.) If the shifter lever won't stay at a particular
setting (i.e. is pulled by the cable), tighten the gear
lever's own adjustment bolt.

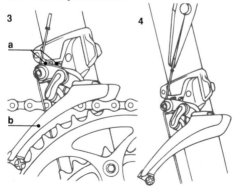

HUB GEARS

A hub gear (**1**), with its gear shifter (**a**) and pulley (**b**) (not found on most modern bikes), has a rear-wheel mechanism (**c**) which is protected from dust, mud and rain inside the hub shell. A three-speed mechanism (**2**) involves four toothed cog wheels. Three, called planetary gears (**a**, **b**, **c**), interact with a central sun wheel (**d**) and a toothed gear ring (**e**) in ways that can vary the rate at which the rear bicycle wheel is made to rotate. You stop pedalling while you change gear. Most hub gears have only three to five speeds, and their main users are cyclists who want to make short trips on sturdy, trouble-free bicycles.

Hub gears need less attention than derailleurs: just regular oiling and maybe adjusting the gear control

1

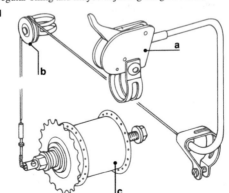

2

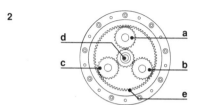

chain (**3**). In a three-speed mechanism this involves
getting into second gear to loosen the cable locknut (**a**)
and screwing the cable connection (**b**) down or up,
stopping when you can see through the inspection
window (**c**) that the end of the indicator rod (**d**) aligns
with the end of the wheel's axle. If a hub gear needs
more than simple adjustment, consult a bicycle shop.
Disassembling the whole mechanism is horrendously
complex and time consuming.

3

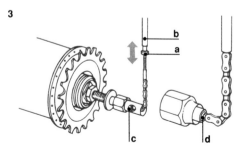

WASHING AND LUBRICATING

Regularly wiping the frame of your bicycle with a
moist cloth removes dust and superficial dirt. To wash
your bicycle, use a sponge and a bucket of warm water
with washing-up liquid. To clean the spokes, rims and
hubs properly, use a soft brush or an old paint brush.
You shouldn't need to dry your bicycle; chemicals in
the washing-up liquid should make it shine.

The sprockets and chain need special attention. Comb
out the dirt between sprockets with a toothbrush.
Remove the chain (see p. 44), soak in paraffin for 12
hours, then (**1**) scrub with a stiff brush, dry, refit and
lubricate. Alternatively, if you want to clean the chain
without removing it, you can buy a special bath (**2**),
which clips over the chain by lifting the back wheel and
turning the pedals, you can run the chain through the
bath to clean it. Lubricating a bicycle protects the steel

1

2

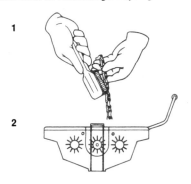

components from rust and reduces friction between moving parts. A synthetic lubricant can defy dirt or water better than ordinary bicycle oil and is less messy. There are synthetic oils you can spray or drip on, and synthetic grease you can squirt from a tube. Ask at a bicycle shop which lubricants meet your needs best and which are compatible. You might have to dissolve away an old lubricant before applying a new one. Always remove excess lubricant: it might collect dirt and make matters worse. Keep lubricants off rims and brake blocks.

Sealed bearings mean that modern bicycles need less oiling or greasing than bicycles made some years ago. Even so, the following items (**3**) need regular oiling or greasing. Oil the chain (**a**). Grease the rear (**b**) and front (**c**) hubs, bottom bracket (**d**) and seat post (**e**). Oil or grease the freewheel (**f**), derailleur (**g**) and exposed cables (**h**).

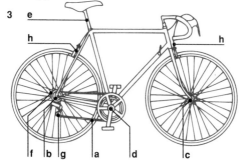

3 e h h f b g a d c

REGULAR MAINTENANCE

Regular maintenance can reveal problems before they develop, and perhaps prevent a breakdown when you may be far from home or a bicycle shop.

Check for the following: (1) misalignment of the frame or broken paint on a steel frame (**a**), caused by a crack in the metal; wheel trueness (**b**); loose or broken spokes (**c**); deformed rims (**d**); split, worn or underinflated tyres (**e**) or thorns, glass or stones needing removal; worn chain (**f**), chainring (**g**), sprockets (**h**) or cables (**i**); and misaligned gears (**j**) or brake blocks (**k**). Check for play on the handlebars (**l**) by trying to turn them with the wheel between your knees. Check for play in the crankset (**m**) by pulling this in and out. Clicking means loose bearings in the bottom bracket; overtight bearings can produce a

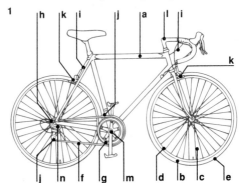

grating sensation when the pedals are spun. However, a fast regular clicking sound from the freewheel (**n**) is normal.

All nuts should be firmly secured: (**2**) fully tighten the saddle clamp (**a**); headset (**b**) if made of steel; cranks' steel lockrings (**c**); axle nuts (**d**) and pedals (**e**). You will probably find that the left pedal tightens anticlockwise. Most other nuts need tightening only until you feel resistance.

Other items to check include the hub and headset bearings. To check for loose headset bearings, stand astride the frame, apply the front brake and rock the bike backwards and forwards. You will be able to see or hear play in the headset. If you lack the time or expertise to carry out this kind of maintenance, get a bicycle shop to do it for you instead. It will cost more, but should give you peace of mind.

2

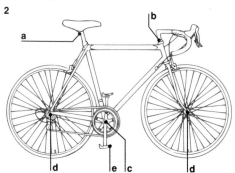

USEFUL EXTRAS: TOOLKIT

A self-reliant cyclist carries tools and spares to cope
with most emergencies. A pump and puncture-repair
outfit are essential. For long trips take additional items.
Spare spokes and cable can be taped onto the frame.

Basic tools

1 Pump that fits the tyre valves
2 Puncture-repair outfit, with tyre levers, big and small
patches, rubber cement and sandpaper. Some kits come
with chalk to powder around a patch to stop cement
sticking to the outer casing
3 Adjustable spanner
4 Screwdrivers (blade and cross-tipped)
5 Pliers
6 Allen (hex) keys to fit recessed hexagonal bolts
7 Spoke key to tighten loose spokes
8 Chain tool (and spare links)
9 Sticky tape (insulating)

Spares

10 Inner tube
11 Spokes and nipples, taped to a seat stay
12 Brake cable (rear length)
13 Gear cable (rear length)
14 Nuts and bolts
15 Light bulbs

For long journeys consider taking additional items such
as lubricants, crank extractor, freewheel remover, hub-
cone spanner and spare brake blocks.

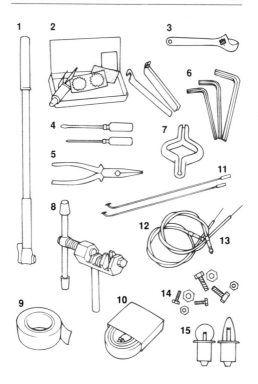

USEFUL EXTRAS: SECURITY AIDS

Bicycle theft is a major problem, so insure your bike.
Mark your postcode on the frame (a bike shop or the
police might help). Make a note of the normally 8–10
digit frame number. Keep your bike indoors where you
can. When you have to leave it outdoors, choose a well-
lit, busy area and lock the frame and rear wheel to a
metal railing or other immovable object. If you have
quick-release wheels, remove the front wheel and lock
that to the frame too.

Bicycle locks come in several types, some more
effective than others. Cable locks (**1**) are slim, flexible,
vinyl-sheathed metal cables. Their advantage is
lightness. Their snag is that they are easily cut by bolt
cutters. Link locks (armoured cable locks) (**2**) are

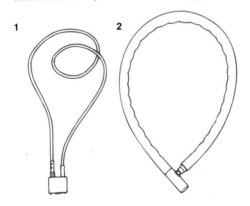

combination locks with a vinyl sheath covering metal links joined by ball-joints. They are flexible and thicker, stronger, heavier and more thief-proof than (**1**). Heavy chain locks (**3**) are another flexible option; motorcycle chains are long enough to loop around the frame and both wheels. U-locks (**4**) are heavy, rigid curved bars made of metal alloy which usually come with a frame-mounted bracket. They defy the efforts of all but very practised thieves.

Other security aids include locks for saddles, pumps and helmets. You can also get battery-powered alarms (**5**). To deter thieves, some people disguise the frame of an expensive new machine with black tape or paint it to make it look not worth stealing.

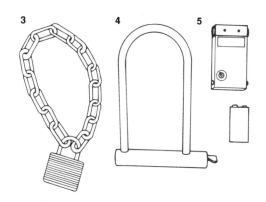

USEFUL EXTRAS: LAMPS AND REFLECTORS

Never cycle at night without being sure you can see and
be seen. Buy a bicycle already equipped with reflectors
(**1**) at the front (**a**), rear (**b**) and on both pedals (**c**).
Spoke reflectors (**d**) are less important, as they only
show up from the side. Wear a reflective belt and put
reflective strips on your luggage (see p.124).
Equip your bike with adequate front and rear lamps.
Battery lamps (**2**) for the front (**a**) and rear (**b**) are easy
to fit (and to remove for security), but most give a
rather weak light, growing weaker as the batteries fade.
Halogen bulbs are brighter than ordinary bulbs, but
fade sooner. Rechargeable battery systems (**3**) consist
of nickel-cadmium or lead-acid batteries, wired to front

1

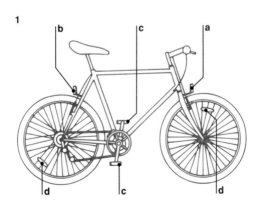

and rear lamps, and a battery recharger to plug into the mains. Rechargeable units produce a far brighter light than ordinary battery lamps but they are costly and some last only an hour before suddenly fading when they need a recharge.

Dynamos (**4**) produce light when a dynamo wheel (**a**) is spun by the rear bicycle wheel. The dynamo generates electricity which flows through wires (**b**) to bulbs in front (**c**) and rear (**d**) lamps. Dynamo lamps give a brighter light than ordinary battery lamps and are cheaper to buy. But they cost more to run, work only when you are moving, produce friction which slightly slows you down and can suffer bulb blowouts unless equipped with a voltage regulator.

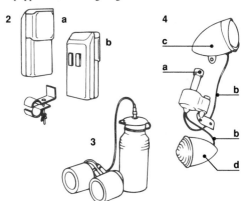

USEFUL EXTRAS: BICYCLE COMPUTERS

Bicycle computers are small, lightweight devices
powered by a long-life battery that display useful
performance data at the touch of a button. They can tell
you exactly how far and how fast you have gone and
much more. Besides being fun to use, computers help
road-racers, time-triallers and anyone cycling for
fitness to keep track of their progress.
Models include the Avocet 30 (**1**), one of the lightest of
all; the Cateye Vectra (**2**), an extremely reliable device;
the Avocet Altimeter 50 (**3**), which shows altitude
climbed; and the Ciclomaster fitness system (**4**).

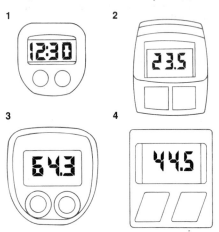

Installation (**5**) of most computers involves mounting a magnet (**a**) on the spokes opposite a sensor (**b**) on the fork; mounting a computer bracket (**c**) on the handlebars; securing a wire (**d**) between sensor and bracket and slotting the computer (**e**) into the bracket. (To prevent theft, remove the computer if leaving your bike unattended.) As the front wheel turns, the magnet passes the sensor and a signal goes to the computer, which calculates the speed. Basic models show current speed, trip distance (journey distance) and time elapsed. Many computers show additional data. This may include average speed, maximum speed reached, total distance since installation, altitude climbed and cadence (pedalling rate). The more functions a computer performs, the more it is likely to cost. Discontinued models can often be the best buys.

5

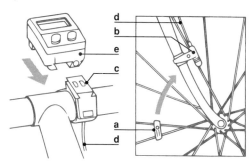

USEFUL EXTRAS: BAGS AND BOTTLES

For everyday use, you can choose from a wide range of small and fairly large bags that attach to the saddle and seat post. A tube bag (**1**) will hold spare inner tubes, basic bicycle tools, keys and valuables. All this and some clothing or shopping will fit into a saddlebag like this aerodynamically-designed, wedge-shaped, five-litre example (**2**). For greater security, some cyclists prefer carrying valuables in a beltbag (**3**).

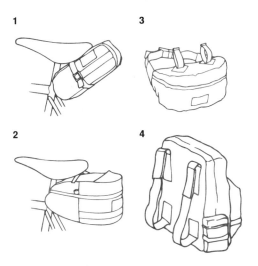

1

3

2

4

Commuters can carry papers and waterproof clothing on their back in a sizable bodybag (**4**) with a rucksack-type harness. But to prevent back strain and an unbalanced ride, it is best to carry heavy loads lower down on the bike itself in panniers or a large saddlebag (see pp. 156–9).

Cycling is thirsty work. Anyone riding more than a few miles should carry a plastic water bottle (**5**) in a lightweight alloy or plastic cage (**6**) attached to the bicycle frame. Bottles with a push-pull valve (**a**) in the lid make it possible to drink as you ride. For long rides in hot weather, you should fit two bottles and consider an extra-large (three-quarters of a litre) size. A zipped Neoprene bottle cover (**7**) will help to keep hot drinks hot and chilled drinks cold.

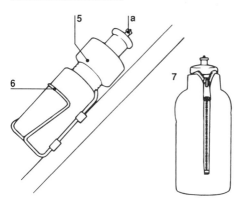

2. Bicycle field guide

BUYING A BICYCLE 1

To buy a new bike, find a bicycle shop that sells the
kind of machine you want (see pp. 68–83), allows a test
ride, and gives a good guarantee and after-sales service.
Choose the right size for you (see pp. 70–1), with
adjustments if necessary.

To buy secondhand, check advertisements in cycling
magazines, or local newspapers or shops. Beware of
stolen or damaged machines, or ones needing costly
repairs. Make sure you check the following items when
buying a secondhand, or new, bike.

From the front (**1**) and rear (**2**), check for frame
straightness (**a**), and alignment of forks (**b**) and wheels
(**c**). Examine the bike from one side (**3**). Crinkly paint
or any repainting where tubes meet on the frame (**a**) or
forks (**b**) might be covering accident damage.

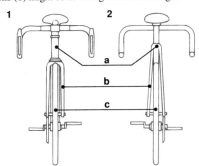

Test various components. Applying the front brake, work the handlebars backwards and forwards. A lot of play might mean a worn headset (**c**). Brake blocks (**d**) should clamp squarely onto the rims (**e**), stopping both wheels at once, and freeing them as you release the brake levers. Check that wheels spin freely, are not buckled, produce no more than 3mm (^{1}/8in) side-to-side movement, and do not click if grasped and pushed sideways. Pluck the spokes (**f**); they should feel taut and go 'plink', not 'plonk'. Check that the tyres are not split or badly worn. Check that cranks (**g**) and pedals (**h**) are not bent, and pedals spin freely. Rocking the cranks reveals unwanted play in the bottom bracket (**i**). Check that you can change through the gears without slippage.

Check bolts, nuts and screws for looseness after buying, and again 80km (50mi) later.

3

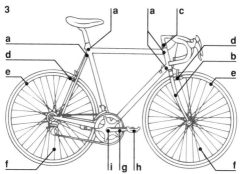

BUYING A BICYCLE 2

Check that the bicycle is the right size for you. Frame
size is fixed, but you can alter some other features.
Specialist firms will even build you a tailor-made
machine, at a price.

Frame size is measured down the seat tube from the
top tube's centre to the bottom bracket's centre (**1**).

1

Choose a frame size 23–25cm (9–10in) less than your
barefooted crotch-to-floor measurement, or 31–33cm
(12–13in) less for a mountain bike, which has a smaller
than standard frame size. If you straddle a standard,
diamond-frame bicycle barefooted, the top tube should
be 2cm (^{3}/4in) below your crotch, or 2.5–5cm (1–2in)
for a mountain bike (**2**). If you must choose between
frames that are bigger or smaller than the ideal size, go
for the smaller frame.
Adjust the saddle height (see p. 23) so that when the
crank is aligned with the seat tube, your lower leg is
straight, but not strained, when your heel, in a low-

heeled shoe, rests on the pedal (**3**). Most people like a
level saddle, but some prefer theirs tilted slightly up or
down.

Adjust the reach so that your fingertips touch the top of
the handlebars when your elbow touches the front of
the saddle (**4**). You may need to move the saddle
forward or back (see p. 23), or buy a handlebar stem
with a longer or shorter reach.

Flat handlebars are usually level with the top of the
saddle and, drop handlebars 2.5cm (1in) lower. You can
raise or lower handlebars slightly (see p. 17).

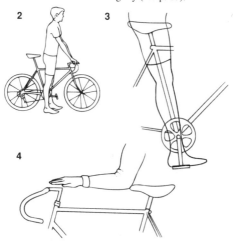

MOUNTAIN BICYCLES

Mountain bikes, alias all-terrain bikes (ATBs), are rugged, lightweight, multigeared, fat-tyred machines (some with front and rear suspension), developed for rough off-road riding and for tackling very steep hills. Their wide, knobbly tyres cope with bumps and mud, but generate friction, making them slow on smooth roads. (Sport, touring and commuting versions have narrower, faster tyres.) Here we show a basic alloy-framed mountain bike (**1**), one with a composite (carbon-fibre/Kevlar) frame (**2**), and a small-wheeled, collapsible variation on the mountain bike theme (**3**). Here are some typical mountain bike specifications:

Weight 9–14kg (21–31lb).

Frame This is smaller than a road bike's, with a high bottom bracket for increased ground clearance. It is made of large-diameter, thick-walled tubing. Typical models have steep head tube angles, a short wheelbase and short chainstays.

Handlebars These are wide and straight, or upswept and angled forward for good control.

Saddle This can be anatomic or semimattress.

Seatpost This is unusually long and dropped by a quick-release lever.

Wheels These usually have a diameter of 66cm (26in) and light alloy rims.

Tyres These are knobbly and up to 54mm ($2^1/_8$in) wide for off-road use; narrower and smoother for road use.

Brakes These can be cantilevers, roller cams or U-brakes.

Cranks These are long, for improved leverage.

Pedals These have sole grips and may have toe-clips and straps.

Gears These are derailleur and wide range with triple chainrings: 15–21 gears for off-road use; usually 10–12 for city use. Handlebar-mounted, indexed thumb shifting gives easy control.
Options Mudguards, etc.

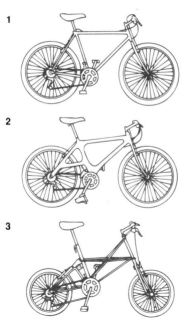

TOURING BICYCLES

The traditional touring bicycle is a strong, fairly light,
long-wheelbase load-bearer. Illustrated are a typical
drop-handlebar design (**1**) and a bike with a mixte
frame (**2**). Many women prefer a mixte frame, but it is
less rigid than the diamond design. For sports tourers,
sports/roadster hybrids, touring mountain bikes and
lightweight mountain bikes see pp. 150–3.

Here are some typical touring bicycle specifications:

Weight 12.25–14.5kg (27–32lb)

Frame This is slightly longer than a racing bicycle's,
with shallower angles and thicker or broader tubing for
added strength. Clips or brazed-on bosses take water
bottles, lighting, racks and mudguards. Long chainstays
prevent too much of the rear panniers' weight falling
behind the back axle.

Handlebars Usually dropped, but shallower and
broader than a racing bike's. Randonneur bars allow a
greater number of riding positions.

Forks Set at a relatively shallow angle giving a
generous clearance between pedals and front wheel, to
allow for mudguards.

Saddle Usually padded and wider than a racing bike's.

Wheels Those with a 65cm (26in) diameter prove
stronger than larger wheels. Quick-release hubs are an
advantage, so are double-butted spokes, as heavy loads
on the rear wheel may cause broken spokes.

Tyres About 28mm ($1^1/_{10}$in) should be the minimum
tyre width on good roads; broader for others.

Brakes The cantilever type is probably best for touring
bicycles, followed by centre-pull brakes.

Pedals Platform pedals are arguably the best, and toe-clips with straps are a good idea.

Gears Touring bicycles typically have 10, 12, 18 or 21 derailleur gears, with a very wide range.

Extras Essential extras include mudguards, racks for panniers, bottles, and lights if riding after dark.

1

2

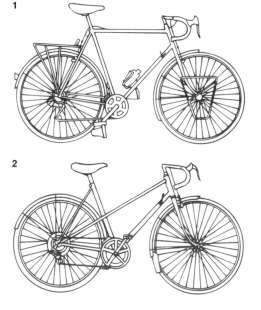

RACING BICYCLES

Racing bicycles are the racehorses and greyhounds of
the cycling world. Their lightweight construction and
streamlined profile help to maximize speed. Various
specialized types appear between pp. 202–17, here we
show a track racer (**1**) and a road racer (**2**).

Here are some basic road-racing bicycle specifications:

Weight 9.5–10kg (21–22lb).

Frame This is shorter than for touring bikes, with
steeper seat and head tubes, and a shorter clearance
between the pedals and front wheel. Such proportions
aid responsiveness and prevent swaying. Many frames
comprise strong, light, steel alloy tubing double-butted
(thickened) at both ends, but new and even lighter
composites are becoming popular.

Handlebars These are dropped to give an efficient,
streamlined riding position.

Wheels Usually aluminium alloy rims and hubs,
stainless-steel spokes, and a quick-release lever.

Tyres These are smooth, 25mm (1in) or even less in
diameter, tubular (cemented on and hard to repair) and
kept highly inflated.

Brakes Side-pull brakes are common on road-racing
bikes (cantilever or roller cams on off-road machines).

Chainset (chainwheels, cranks, bottom bracket
bearings) Usually matched products from one maker.

Pedals Traditional quill cage pedals have toe-clips and
straps, and system pedals accept shoe cleats, which
riders lock onto by stepping into them.

Gears The derailleur gears have a narrower range than
touring bikes' gears and maybe no more than seven
speeds. Top-road racing cyclists make do with a very

narrow spread. The shift levers are mounted on the down tube of the bicycle frame.
Extras Racing bikes are stripped to the minimum. Road-racers lack such things as mudguards, carriers and lights. Track bikes even lack gears and brakes.

1

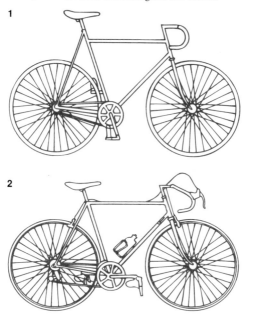

2

SMALL-WHEELED BICYCLES

These include a wide range of bicycles with antler, flat,
or dropped handlebars, and have only small wheels in
common. Their main advantage is small size for easy
storage, especially those machines that fold up and fit
in a cupboard, car boot or carrying bag. Instability and
vulnerability to potholes can be a problem. Cheap
models tend to be heavy, ungeared and hard work. The
best-engineered small-wheelers are geared, lightweight,
and handle well, but they can be extremely expensive.

1 Basic small-wheeled shoppers weigh up to 20.4kg
(45lb). These heavy machines have open frames of
broad-diameter tubing and room for a large load on a
rear luggage rack. Versions with a hinged frame can be
folded in half. Broad tyres with thick treads damp down
the jolting that small wheels tend to accentuate, but fat
tyres create a huge rolling resistance. Ungeared bikes
like this are heavy going. Short shopping trips are their
practical limit.

2 Bickerton bicycles include 3-speed alloy machines
(**a**) weighing only 10kg (22lb), and collapsing into an
easily portable form (**b**).

3 Moulton bicycles are sophisticated lightweight small-
wheelers, weighing only 10.9kg (24lb). They first
appeared in the early 1960s, with a revolutionary frame
featuring a web of slim rods and braces (innovations
include corrosion-proof stainless-steel tubing). There is
independent front and rear wheel suspension. Tyres are
narrow and fast, and multigear options are available.
Instead of folding this kind of bicycle, you use a key to
split it in two.

1

2

a

b

3

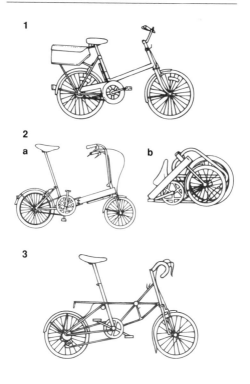

TANDEMS

Tandems are two-rider machines for a 'captain', or pilot, and a 'stoker'. The captain steers the front wheel and controls brakes and gears. There are touring (**1**), mountain (**2**) and lightweight racing versions. Tandems possess several advantages over single-rider machines. A typical lightweight tandem weighs only three-quarters as much as two bicycles and creates only half as much wind resistance. This means that two on a tandem can ride faster than if they rode separately. Freewheeling downhill is very fast indeed. Other benefits include being able to chat with less risk than riding side by side. There are disadvantages, though. A tandem takes less luggage than two bicycles, and the combined weights of the tandem and its riders, plus its long wheelbase, make climbing hills hard work. Here are some basic tandem specifications:

Weight 15.9–29.9kg (35–66lb).

Frame This is heavy and the wheelbase is very long. Various frame designs (**3**) are used to prevent 'whip' and maximize the output of riders of equal and unequal muscle power. A double marathon frame (**a**) is suited to riders of equal strength, a direct lateral frame (**b**) is better for riders of unequal strength.

Handlebars These comprise two pairs of dropped or straight bars. The captain's handlebars steer the front wheel, and the stoker's provide only support.

Forks These are thick, for extra support.

Wheels These have extra-strong rims and hubs, and additional (up to 48) spokes to withstand the great weight.

Tyres may be as much as 54mm ($2^1/_{10}$ in) wide, and must be very highly inflated to support two riders.
Brakes Powerful cantilever brakes with an extra disc or drum brake control speed while the tandem is freewheeling downhill.
Pedals These comprise two pairs linked by a chain on the left side of the frame – a so-called crossover drive.
Gears The derailleur gears are controlled by the captain. Extra low and high gears are needed for uphill and downhill work.

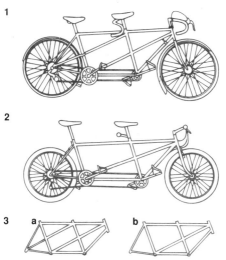

1

2

3   a   b

TRICYCLES FOR ADULTS

Tricycles are three-wheeled machines with a broad-based support. Most have one wheel in front and a wheel on each side of the saddle. Unlike a bicycle, tricycles require no balancing skill at slow speed, and remain standing when stationary. Adults' tricycles include machines used for shopping and transporting young children (1), lightweight tourers and racing machines (2), and recreational recumbents (p. 244). Solidly built, load-bearing tricycles (3) are used as mobile shops, for transport in warehouses, as wheelbarrows, and (especially in the developing world) as vans and trishaw taxis.

A tricycle's stability makes it safer than a bicycle on a slippery road and for people suffering impaired balance. But it handles differently from a bicycle. You must turn the handlebars more to steer around corners, and, on a lightweight machine, at the same time shift your body weight to prevent a wheel lifting. Pedalling a tricycle can take up to 10 per cent more effort than pedalling a bicycle. The other main problem is finding space to park and store your machine.

1

Here are some basic tricycle specifications:

Weight 19–45kg (42–100lb).

Frame This involves additional tubing.

Wheels These normally comprise one steerable front wheel and two rear wheels fixed to a long axle. Most tricycles have small 50cm (20in) wheels, giving a low centre of gravity, which enhances stability. Touring and racing machines have wheels as large as a full-size bicycle's.

Brakes These may be on the front wheel only, or on all three wheels.

Gears These vary from a single fixed gear to a wide-range derailleur system.

2

3

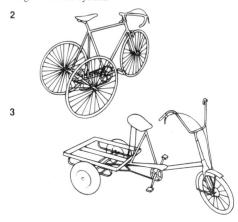

CHILD SEATS AND TRAILERS

Children aged under six are too young to ride very far
on their own, but they can travel with the family as
bicycle passengers, thanks to child seats and child
trailers. From about six years old they can also pedal a
trailer bicycle attached to a full-size machine.

1 Children aged between 10 months and 4 years can sit
in a rear-mounted, one-piece plastic seat, with head
restraint, safety bar, safety straps, spoke guards for feet,
and mountings for attachment over the rear wheel.
Crash helmets and, in cool weather, warm windproof
clothing to prevent chilling are essentials.

2 A child trailer is a stable, low-slung rear attachment
with two wheels, comfortable seat and tyres, and a
detachable weatherproof hood. Trailers can take two
small children, the elder aged up to five. They are more
stable attachments than child seats.

3 Trailer bicycles are rear attachments to full-size
bicycles. They look like a child's bicycle without the
front wheel. The child sits on a low saddle, gripping
handlebar supports and pedalling the small rear wheel
of what, in effect, becomes a three-wheeled 'tandem'.
Rather like a pair on a tandem, the adult and the child
cyclist benefit from an overall reduction in wind
resistance and an increase in power. Trailer bicycles are
best for children aged 6 to 10.

A complex extension of the trailer bicycle concept is
the bicycle train: a tricycle with added child seats,
followed in succession by two, two-wheeled trailers
linked one behind the other. This arrangement can carry
two parents, two infants and one older child.

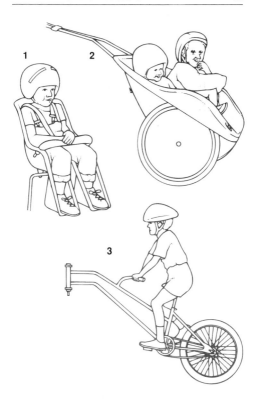

CHILDREN'S BICYCLES

As with adults' bicycles, quality matters, and children's bicycles must be the right sizes for their riders: too large ('a bike to grow into') and the rider will wobble.

1 Tricycles These are best for children aged about 2 to 4. The smallest models have pedals attached to the front wheel. The best children's tricycles feature inflatable tyres, a chaindrive, chainguard and brakes. Young children tricycling outdoors need good brakes and constant supervision.

2 Small-framed, small-wheeled bicycles These bikes, with a chainguard and steel (not plastic) ball bearings suit children aged 4 to 7. Some experts suggest detaching such bicycles' stabilizers, and encouraging children to learn to balance by scooting along, with the pedals removed.

3 BMX ('bicycle motocross') bicycles These are small-framed, small-wheel, off-road machines, with a low saddle, high, wide handlebars, fat, knobbly tyres, and a single, low gear. Well-built BMX bikes are sturdy enough to climb curbs, perform stunts, leap hillocks and execute airborne jumps. They are great fun for children aged at least 7. The best bikes are expensive.

4 Junior mountain bikes These are designed for children aged 8 to 12, have flat handlebars, indexed gear-shifting and knobbly tyres like the full-sized versions, but smaller frames and fewer derailleur gears.

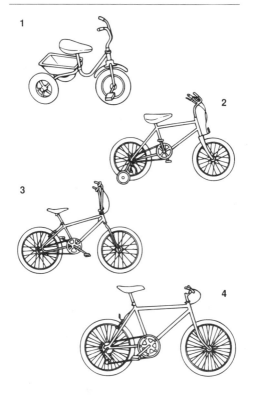

1

2

3

4

CITY BICYCLES

Various modified and 'hybrid' bicycles find a place in the modern city, whether used by shoppers, commuters, messengers or patrolling police. Hybrid mountain machines have largely ousted the rest.

1 Light roadster Typically this has a wide saddle (**a**), flat handlebars (**b**) giving an upright riding position, fairly broad tyres (**c**), three hub gears (**d**), mudguards (**e**) and maybe a chainguard (**f**). It weighs about 16kg (35lb) and is useful for short trips and shopping.

1

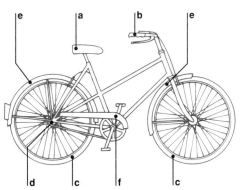

2 The sports/roadster hybrid This has a roadster's wide saddle (**a**), flat handlebars (**b**), upright riding position, mudguards (**c**), calliper brakes worked by hand levers (**d**) and a carrier (**e**); components are light, tyres fairly narrow (**f**) and there are usually five derailleur gears (**g**). Such bikes weigh about 12–15kg (26–33lb). They are suitable for commuting and the occasional longer ride.

2

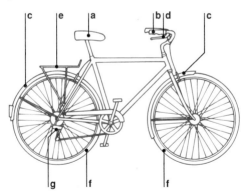

3 Hybrid mountain bike This has the flat, straight
handlebars (**a**) and indexed gear-shifting (**b**) of a
normal mountain bike, but lighter components and
narrower, faster tyres (**c**) than an off-road machine, also
often a lower bottom bracket (**d**), and quite likely only
10 to 12 derailleur gears (**e**). Commuters, messengers
and the police increasingly favour such bikes.

3

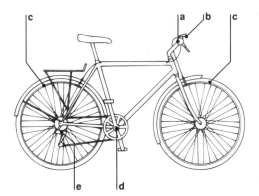

4 Sports bike This includes some features seen in drop-handlebar touring and racing machines. It has a narrow saddle (**a**), dropped handlebars (**b**), a lightweight frame (**c**), fairly narrow tyres (**d**) and 10 to 12 derailleur gears (**e**). It weighs about 13kg (29lb). Sports bikes give a livelier ride than sports/roadster hybrids and tackle hills better.

4

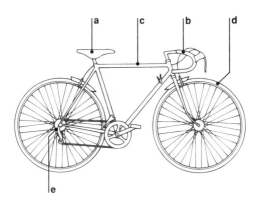

HEAVY ROADSTERS AND UTILITY BICYCLES

These are durable bicycles designed for reliability and carrying loads, not for high-speed performance.

1 Heavy roadsters These are sturdily built machines, weighing 18–23kg (40–50lb). They have a strong steel frame (**a**), broad saddle (**b**), 'sit-up-and-beg' handlebars (**c**), rod brakes (**d**), wide rims and tyres (**e**), and generous mudguards (**f**). Many come with a chain-guard (**g**) and a carrier over the rear wheel. There may be one gear or three hub gears, and perhaps a hub dynamo and a shopping basket attached to the

1

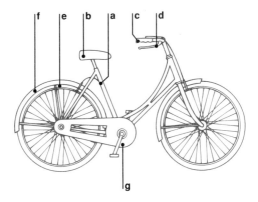

handlebars. Heavy roadsters have largely disappeared in the West, but they remain the chief means of personal transport in many Asian and African countries.
2 Utility bikes These are the single-speed, North American equivalent of the heavy roadster. Features include 'longhorn' handlebars (**a**), wide tyres (**b**) and a coaster brake (**c**) which stops the rear wheel when you back-pedal. Utility bikes are the paperboy's traditional delivery bike and, with wire baskets, can carry enough groceries for a small family. These bikes inspired the similar-looking beach cruisers for recreational off-road use, with or without mudguards and derailleur gears.

2

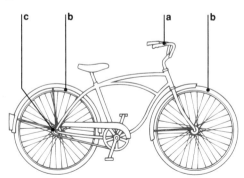

SPECIAL BICYCLES AND TRICYCLES

Human-powered machines offer opportunities for
transport and exercise to people with a wide range of
physical problems. Carefully chosen types of bicycle
are good enough to cancel out the effects of some
disabilities. Individuals unable to swing a leg high
enough to mount a bike with a crossbar can mount a
bicycle with an open frame. A one-legged cyclist has
climbed the highest mountain pass in Europe on a
normal bicycle equipped with extremely low gears.
Cyclists with impaired balance may cope on tricycles,
which they can stop at junctions or on steep hills
without fear of falling off. Blind cyclists can ride as
stokers on tandems with sighted captains.

A simple modification to a bicycle can overcome
certain disabilities. A person with a misaligned foot (**1**)
can easily build a wedge on a pedal (**2**), or else inside a
shoe. A platform built up on one pedal compensates if
one leg is shorter than the other. Unusually short cranks
let stiff-jointed riders pedal with only the minimum of
joint movement.

1   **2**

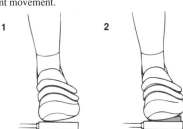

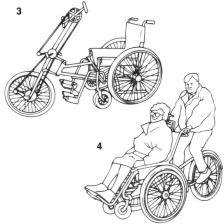

Special machines can even help people confined to wheelchairs. Adding an arm-powered pedal-adapter kit with an extra-low gear derailleur system to the front of a wheelchair, produces a tricycle (**3**). A fairly strong person can power this along using their arms on level ground and up and down gentle hills, back-pedalling to brake. Not all wheelchair-bound people can manage this. But attaching a different device onto the back of a wheelchair converts this into a tricycle, with a rider seated behind the wheelchair to pedal the chair and its occupant (**4**).

'FUN' BICYCLES

Children's tricycles, BMX machines, mountain bikes, and beach cruisers provide transport as well as amusement, but some machines were built purely for fun. Ingenious inventors have produced astonishing variations on the theme of pedal power, for their own amusement, or to amaze spectators at circuses and carnivals. Here are just a few examples.

1 Five-rider bicycle Designers have built bicycles for even more riders than this. In 1979, no fewer than 35 cyclists rode the longest-ever bike, a Belgian machine more than 20m (66ft) long.

2 The world's smallest six-pedal bicycle: a Swiss machine 48cm (19in) long.

3 Unicycle Such unstable, one-wheeled machines call for very skilful balancing. One rider managed to ride a unicycle more than 31m (nearly 102ft) high over a distance of more than 100m (328ft).

4 Double-decker tandem A Japanese invention 5m (16ft 5in) long and 3.4m (11ft 1¹/₅in) high to the upper handlebars.

1

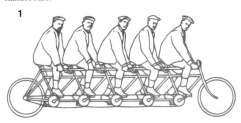

3. The cyclist

LEARNING TO RIDE

There is more than one way to master riding an unstable two-wheeled machine. Of the three ways shown here, experts consider the third is by far the best.

1 Riding a bicycle fitted with small stabilizing wheels gives the learner little idea of how to balance.

2 Riding a bicycle while someone runs behind you supporting the saddle and then lets go can be an unnerving experience for the learner. Beginners are liable to lose confidence and topple over when they realize that their support is no longer there. Even so, perhaps most cyclists learnt to ride in this way.

3 A third option is sitting on a bicycle with the pedals removed and the saddle lowered enough for the rider to stand with both feet on the ground. The rider pushes along, using alternate feet, and getting the feel of the brakes. The next stage (**4**) is pushing along with both feet together, then raising the feet and freewheeling a

1

short distance, then going further by freewheeling down a short, gentle slope. Once riders can balance like this they can move on to the last stage: simultaneous balancing and pedalling. Replace the pedals, raise the saddle a bit and let the rider freewheel down a gentle slope with both feet on the pedals, then encourage the rider to start pedalling at the foot of the slope.

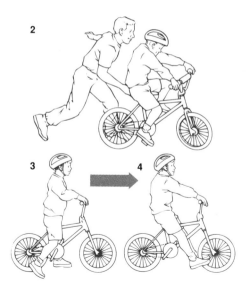

BASIC RIDING TECHNIQUES

Effective cycling involves achieving a sound riding
position. On a flat-handlebar bike, sit with most of your
weight on the seat (**1**) but not bolt upright. For a drop-
handlebar bike lean forward so that nearly half your
weight rests on the handlebars (**2**) without the need to
stretch your arms fully. If your bike is incorrectly sized,
simply adjusting the saddle and handlebars, and/or
replacing the handlebar stem may be enough to achieve
the right posture. If not you might need a bike that fits
your own measurements better (see p. 70). Next (**3**),
practise effective pedalling, exerting pressure on each
pedal with the ball of the foot (**a**) not the instep or the
toes. Pedalling with the ball of the foot makes the most
of the leg's role as a lever (**b**).

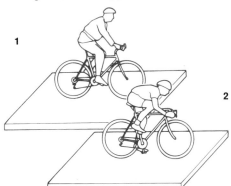

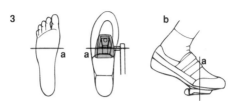

Traffic-free parks or playgrounds are suitable places to learn road-riding skills. Start with the bike in low gear, the right pedal forward and raised. Sit on the bike, with your right foot on the right pedal and your left foot on the ground. Look behind carefully as you would on a road to check all is clear. Push off and start pedalling. Change into a higher gear as you accelerate. Practise steering between two parallel chalk lines (**4**), 10cm (4in) apart, marked on the ground. When you can do this without touching the lines, halve the gap between the lines. When you can steer between the narrowed gap, halve it again.

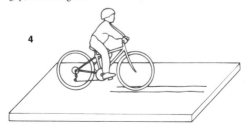

CORNERING

Trying to corner by simply steering with the handlebars
will unbalance you. A cyclist must lean into a right-
hand bend to counter the centripetal force tending to
pitch the rider off to the left, and vice versa. Successful
turning usually involves simply leaning the bicycle and
rider into a bend (**1**), and making only very slight
steering adjustments. The faster your speed and the
harder you lean, the tighter the turn you will make,
although leaning too steeply could capsize you,
especially on loose gravel. Corner with the pedal on the
inside of the bend raised to prevent it hitting the
ground. When the turn is completed, oversteering into
the bend brings your body's centre of gravity back over
the bike, allowing you to assume a new straight course.
At low speed you can turn more sharply by making
your bike lean more steeply than your body (**2**).
Performed in low gear, this is a useful tactic if you have
to perform a U-turn in a narrow road, but stop and

1

make sure the road is clear first. Otherwise, get off and walk to the other side. At high speed the opposite occurs: you can reduce the turn's radius by leaning your body more steeply than your bike (**3**).

Experienced cyclists sometimes use a special technique in making tight turns. As they approach a turn, they steer the bike away from the turn, sharply tilting it over into the turn. They then steer into the turn to avoid losing balance, then oversteer before correcting as normal. This manoeuvre is mostly used in racing to maintain speed at turns. It can be a useful way to avoid road hazards. However, it is dangerous at high speed and in traffic, and should not be attempted by inexperienced cyclists. In risky situations always put safety first – slow down or stop if necessary.

2   **3**

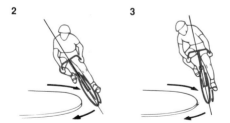

SIGNALLING AND LOOKING BACK

A vital aid to safety on busy roads is giving a clear
hand signal of your intentions when you come to a
junction or want to stop. If you are moving, this leaves
only one hand for steering. Practise one-handed
steering well away from traffic (for instance in a quiet
park), by lifting your right hand and holding it away
from your body while you steer with the left hand,
learning to compensate for the shift in your centre of
gravity. Then reverse the roles of both hands.

When you can steer one-handed, practise looking
behind to check that the road is safe for you to signal an
intended manoeuvre. Steering with the left hand, look
back over your right shoulder (**1**), letting your right
hand trail slightly behind you. Repeat, looking back
over your left shoulder. Steering straight with one-hand
while looking back is extremely difficult, and risky if

1

2

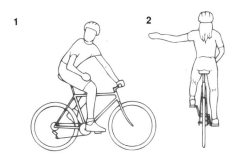

traffic is heavy. A quick glance with both hands on the handlebars is safer, but reveals less. Unfortunately, a mirror is no substitute for a good backward look. The mirror's vibration and limited field of view, and the time lost refocusing your eyes, may limit a mirror's use to showing you only when it is safe to turn your head. There are four basic hand signals. To signal a left turn (**2**), hold your left arm out horizontally to the left. To signal a right turn (**3**), hold your right arm out horizontally to the right. To signal slowing down (**4**), move your right arm up and down. To signal straight ahead, at a crossroads for example, raise your right-hand with the palm forward (**5**).

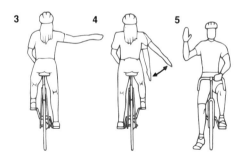

SLOWING DOWN AND STOPPING

Get the feel of how squeezing the brake levers operates
your brakes. As you brake be sure to steer straight.
Gently squeezing the left-hand brake lever retards the
rear wheel enough to slow you down gently in traffic,
or on a slight downhill slope. For firmer braking, apply
both brakes. Start applying the back brake a moment
before the front brake. The front brake has the greater
stopping power, but fiercely slamming it on can pitch a
rider over the handlebars. In an emergency stop, move
your body backward, shifting your weight onto the
pedals to improve stability by lowering the centre of
gravity (**1**). But applying both brakes at high speed may
risk locking the wheels and send you into a skid. Your
speed and alertness, as well as road and weather
conditions, all affect braking distance. (**2**) On a dry
road, at 15mph (**a**) the stopping distance is nearly twice
that for 10mph (**b**). (**3**) In wet weather both distances
(**c**, **d**) are more than doubled. (**4**) Down a wet 1 in 10

1

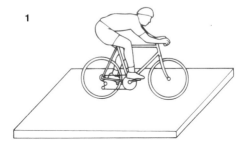

slope, a tired cyclist going 15mph takes nearly twice as far to stop (**e**) as one going 10mph (**f**), and six times as far as an alert rider at 10mph on a flat road in dry weather. In wet weather, you should often lightly apply the brakes to rid the rims of water. On long downhill runs, pump the brakes on and off to slow down safely. Synthetic brake blocks on alloy rims are more effective in the wet than rubber blocks on steel rims. All brakes must be properly adjusted to work efficiently.

You can often slow down and stop with minimal use of your brakes. First, change down into a low gear, especially if you will remount going up a hill. In heavy traffic, give the slowing down signal, squeeze the brakes gently at the last moment, and stop close enough to the roadside to set one foot on the kerb or verge.

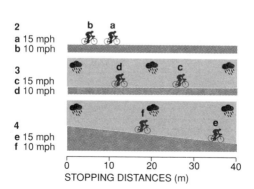

2
a 15 mph
b 10 mph

3
c 15 mph
d 10 mph

4
e 15 mph
f 10 mph

0   10   20   30   40
STOPPING DISTANCES (m)

RIDING IN TRAFFIC

A bicycle has as much right on the road as a bus, and
safe cycling includes asserting that right. The general
rule is to ride about 1m (3ft) from the kerb (**1**), so other
drivers can clearly see you and you can avoid drain
covers, broken glass and being boxed in behind parked
vehicles. If the traffic is heavy you might have to move
closer in to let lorries pass, and of course cyclists
should ride in single file, as riding two abreast would
prevent other vehicles overtaking. Overtaking on a
bicycle requires special care. Prepare to overtake a
parked vehicle well in advance (**2**): check for following
vehicles, signal and move right in your own traffic lane,
check again, then signal and pull out further to
overtake, leaving a gap in case a door on the vehicle
you are passing suddenly opens.

In slow-moving traffic, keep in the main flow and stay
well behind other vehicles: their brakes are more

1

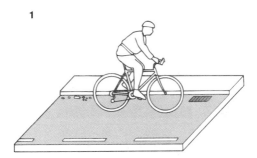

powerful than yours. Overtaking lorries on the inside is extremely dangerous, because the drivers cannot normally see you. In stop-go traffic, get into a low gear and try to slow down without stopping in order to maintain your momentum and place in the flow. If you must stop, stop in the middle of the left-hand lane, where drivers can clearly see you.

2

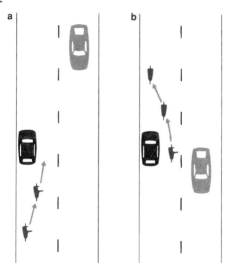

AT JUNCTIONS AND ROUNDABOUTS

1 To make a left turn Keep away from the edge of the road, signal just before turning, and watch out for other vehicles and pedestrians.

2 To make a right turn into a minor road Choose a break in the following traffic, signal, move almost into

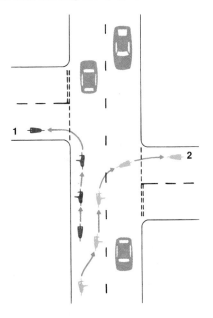

the middle of the road, and change down. If there is nothing coming, make a right-angled turn into the minor road's left-hand lane. Otherwise, wait opposite the middle of the minor road, not blocking the flow. On narrow or busy roads, it is sometimes safer not to wait in the middle of the road before turning right. Instead, pull over to the side of the road and wait until a break in the traffic – both on the main road and on the road you want to turn into – allows you to complete your turn in one manoeuvre.

3 To make a right turn from a minor road into a major road Signal, move to the right of your lane as before, change down and wait at the junction. When all is clear, signal and cross over before turning right.

3

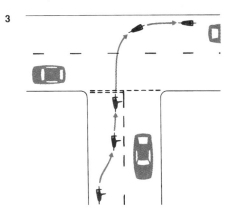

At a single-lane roundabout Change down and give
way to traffic circulating from the right. To turn left (**4**),
maintain your usual kerb distance. To ride straight
ahead (**5**), position yourself in the middle of your lane
and stay there as you cycle across. To turn right (**6**),
stay just right of the middle. In each case, signal left
before leaving the roundabout.

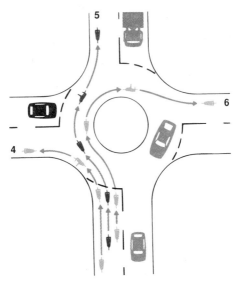

SPECIAL SITUATIONS

At a four-lane crossroads Do not attempt to cross a busy four-lane crossroads on your bike. It is only safe if all the lanes are clear, and this might take forever! If there are traffic lights and a pedestrian crossing, walk across when the lights are in your favour. If there are no lights, turn left when the way is clear and cross on foot at the next pedestrian crossing (**1**).

1

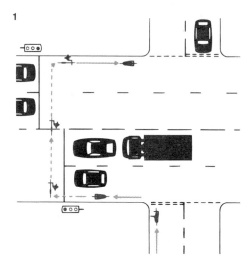

If there are traffic lights, ride straight across, signalling, and wait in the far lane (**2**) for oncoming traffic to pass.

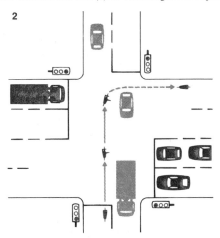

At a multi-lane roundabout Change down and give way to circulating traffic coming from your right. To go straight ahead (**3**), leave room for vehicles to overtake on your right. To go left (**4**), stay on the left, signal and exit. To turn right (**5**), manoeuvre into the outer lane, and circulate in that position, pedalling fast, if the traffic is heavy, just on the left of vehicles close to the roundabout centre. Before your exit, signal clearly and begin to peel off.

In tricky traffic situations, making eye contact with a driver might encourage him or her to give way, but always expect risky behaviour by other road users: overtaking cars that cut in; parked vehicles that start as you pass; articulated lorries swinging into your path to make a tight turn; oncoming cars overtaking on your side of the road; incautious pedestrians; startled horses; dogs straying onto the road. In some situations it is safer – and quicker – to get off and walk.

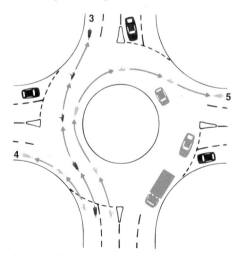

BICYCLE PATHS

In some bicycle-friendly parts of the world, cyclists no longer have to jostle for road space with fast, heavy vehicles. Instead, they can ride safely apart from more dangerous traffic. In certain cities (**1**), a bicycle symbol and a painted line on the road mark an inner lane which cyclists share only with buses and taxis (**a**); on some wide, busy roads the line marks off a bicycle lane banned even to these (**b**). Be careful on such lanes, as they often end abruptly before junctions. There are also purpose-built bicycle paths and bridges (**2**).

1

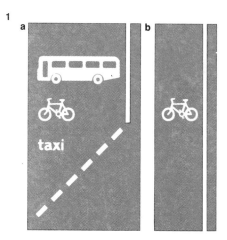

The United States has a number of bicycle routes. In Europe, a complex network of bikeways crisscrosses the Netherlands. Belgium, Denmark and Germany also have bicycle paths. Compared to these countries, the United Kingdom still has a poor record of providing bicycle routes. However, the charity Sustrans (short for 'Sustainable Transport') has begun to develop a network of traffic-free routes linking cities.

2

COPING WITH HAZARDS

Apart from other road users, the road itself is the cause
of most of the hazards a cyclist may encounter. In
places the road surface is defective. A few old streets
consist of bone-jarring cobbles. Far more common
problems are (**1**) bumps (**a**) and potholes, including
deep craters hidden beneath benign-looking puddles
(**b**). There are also permanent hazards inserted into the
road, especially raised manhole covers (**c**), and gratings
or railway lines that can snare a bicycle wheel.
Temporary dangers that lie on the surface range from
gravel and thorny hedge cuttings to broken glass (**d**),
metal fragments that have fallen off vehicles, and
slippery films of oil, water and ice.

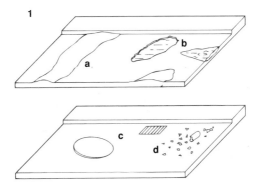

To cope with threats like these, keep an eye on the road
surface at least 15m (about 50ft) ahead, further if riding
fast. This allows time to check that traffic conditions
are safe for riding out around an obstacle. If not, you
can clear a pothole or bump by approaching the hazard
head-on, standing in the saddle, hauling the handlebars
up, and then leaning forward as your front wheel comes
down on the far side. The same head-on jumping
technique may help you clear a shallow, narrow trench
cut across the road. At level crossings, cross the railway
lines squarely (**2**). To traverse a slippery patch, steer
steadily in a straight line and avoid braking. Ride over
cobbles by gripping your handlebars hard.

2

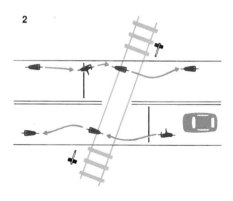

CYCLING ACCIDENTS

Accidents kill thousands of cyclists a year, hundreds in the United Kingdom alone. In 1991, for example, more than 240 UK cyclists died, and another 3900 were seriously injured, nearly one-third of them children. Far more car drivers than cyclists were killed, but statistics show that riding a bicycle is much riskier than driving a car. In the UK, in 1990, for every 100 million kilometres travelled, 501 cyclists were killed or injured compared to 34 car drivers. This is hardly surprising, for cyclists are inconspicuous and ride unstable machines, with no outer shell to protect them against fast-moving cars, trucks or buses.

One British survey (1) showed that most cycling accidents happen at or near junctions. A United States survey (2) blamed other vehicles for no more than 10 per cent of all cycling accidents. Where no motor vehicle was involved, research reveals that most riders simply fall off (3). Even so, most accidents happen mainly to careless or inexperienced riders and could be avoided by obeying the highway code, and looking and planning ahead, especially at junctions, where catching a motorist's eye can help make your intentions clear.

> Always be extremely aware of motorists. Try to make eye contact whenever possible, and expect the worst of drivers, i.e. pulling out of side roads or turning left after overtaking. You won't be able to fully anticipate drunk drivers and inattentive drivers, so in general, always be ALERT and ASSERTIVE.

1 Where accidents happen

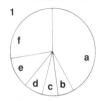

a At T or staggered junctions: 42%
b At other junctions: 6%
c At private entrances: 6%
d At roundabouts: 7%
e At crossroads: 11%
f More than 20m (about 66ft) from a junction: 28%

2 Causes of accidents

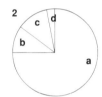

a Cyclist error: 75%
b Vehicle driver error: 10%
c Defective bicycle: 12%
d Defective road: 3%

3 Accidents without motor vehicles

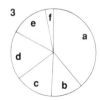

a Cyclists fell off: 39%
b Cyclists hit something: 12%
c Cyclists cornered or rode downhill too fast: 14%
d Cyclists performed stunts: 18%
e Cyclists lost control: 14%
f Other causes: 4%

AVOIDABLE ACCIDENTS

Here we explain 10 common causes of accidents, most of which an alert cyclist could prevent or avoid.

1 A cyclist rides into a street from a drive or a minor road without looking first, and is hit by a car.

2 A cyclist turns right without checking that it is safe to do so, and is hit by a following car.

3 A cyclist suddenly swerves out around an obstruction, and is hit by a following car.

4 A cyclist rides too close to a line of parked cars and is knocked over when a car door suddenly opens.

5 A cyclist runs into the back of a vehicle that has suddenly stopped.

6 A cyclist riding wide in poor light without adequate lights is hit by a following car.

7 An oncoming car turns right at a crossroads, unsighted by traffic, and into the cyclist's path.

8 Just after overtaking a cyclist, a vehicle turns left into a side road, obstructing the cyclist's path.

9 A driver stops at a busy crossroads, sees an apparent break in the traffic and accelerates into a passing cyclist.

10 A vehicle (or pedestrian, cat or dog) obscured by a parked vehicle suddenly moves out into the road, and into the cyclist's path.

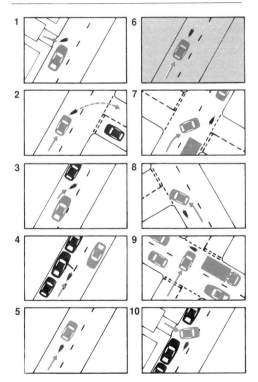

SAFETY AIDS

Many cycling injuries happen because the driver of a
vehicle hits a cyclist without noticing the bike and its
rider. Apart from riding safely, your best hope of
preventing accidents is making sure that buses, cars,
and trucks can see that you are there. (**1**) Wearing a pale
shirt, cycling jersey or jacket (**a**) makes you more
conspicuous than drab-coloured clothing, especially in
dim or fading light. Wearing a reflective belt or sash (**b**)
also helps to draw attention to a cyclist. Some cyclists
feel safest with a yellow plastic spacer flag (**c**) stuck out
sideways from their bikes. Other aids include reflective
strips on the backs of panniers (**d**) and reflective pedals
(**e**), as well as the bicycle's own lamps and front and
rear reflectors. However, be sure your visual aids show
clearly what and where you are: too many gimmicks
can be confusing.

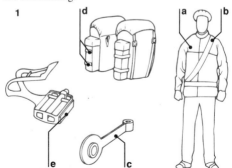

As for making warning sounds, some safety experts
think a warning shout is more effective than a bell.
Even the best safety precautions will not always
prevent an accident, but injury may be limited if
cycling gloves and helmets are worn. (More than half
of all major cycling injuries involve injuring the head.
Some nations now ban cycling without helmets.
Helmets come in several varieties. The foam-strip 'hair-
net' helmet (**2**) offers minimal protection. Safer
versions include the hard-shell helmet (**3**) with a shock-
absorbent liner, and the soft-shell helmet (**4**) with
a shock-absorbent liner and fabric cover. Choose a
helmet that is strong, well-ventilated, lightweight and
fits snugly. But remember, visibility, a mechanically
sound bike and alertness are all equally important.

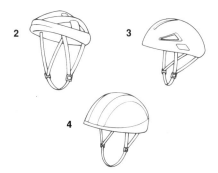

CYCLING INJURIES

Accidents happen even to careful cyclists.
A rider falling on a hard surface is likely to suffer
minor scratches and cuts. (**1**) To treat an abrasion (**a**)
wash the wound with soap and water, (**b**) clean out dirt
and swab the skin with antiseptic solution. If necessary,
cover the wound with a sterile dressing (**c**), applied by
pulling its plastic tabs sideways. However, most
abrasions heal fastest left exposed to the air. To be on
the safe side, have an antitetanus injection, unless you
completed a course less than two years before, and see
a doctor if the wound swells or you feel feverish.
Putting out a hand as you fall can damage ligaments,
producing a sprained wrist, with swelling and
discoloration. (**2**) Bandage the wrist, starting with one
horizontal turn (**a**). Pull the bandage diagonally across
the palm in front of the thumb (**b**), then around the back

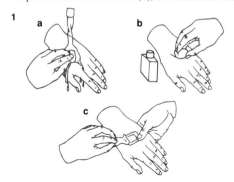

of the hand, across the palm and around the wrist (**c**). Repeat (**b**) and (**c**) until you have supported the wrist without impairing the hand's blood supply. Test this by pressing a fingernail until it turns white. When you stop pressing, the nail should turn pink. If not, the bandage is too tight. Besides wrists, cyclists sometimes sprain knees or ankles. If touching or moving the injured part causes stinging pain or you run a high temperature, the 'sprain' might be a fracture and requires medical help. Wrist and collarbone fractures are the most common breaks suffered by cyclists. If someone falls on their head they may suffer concussion, perhaps a fractured skull, and even brain damage. Telephone for an ambulance, if possible.

2

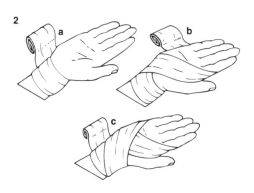

CYCLING AILMENTS

Cycling improves overall health, but cyclists are liable to various, mainly mild, ailments (**1**). Most of these are relieved by adjusting the rider's bicycle, clothing or cycling habits.

Backache and neck ache (**a**) may be relieved by raising the handlebars and shortening the gap between them and your saddle. Try to avoid saddle soreness (**b**) by wearing seamless-crotch cycling shorts, and washing these and your crotch after each ride. If soreness occurs, applying alcohol and talcum powder to sore skin may bring relief, and you should consider getting a wider, softer saddle. On a long ride, steady pressure can numb the crotch (**c**), feet (**d**), or hands (**e**). Relieve these by rising in the saddle from time to time; wearing stiff-soled shoes with a cushioned insole; and changing hand positions (easiest on a drop-handlebar bike); wearing cycling gloves; and fitting padded handlebar covers. Cycling in too high a gear can cause painful knees (**f**) and inflamed Achilles tendons (**g**). Use lower gears and, if necessary, rest. Painful knees can also result from prolonged riding with the saddle set too low.

Breathing in cold air through the mouth can cause sinus (**h**) and bronchial (**i**) ailments: in chilly air breathe through the nose (go slower if necessary) and protect your chest. Getting chilled right through brings a risk of hypothermia, with uncontrolled shivering, clumsiness, confused thought – even death. Prevent it by dressing warmly (including the feet and hands) and taking hot drinks. In hot weather, overheating, sunburn and dehydration are problems. Apply a high-protection sun cream, wear a brimmed hat and light clothing, and drink plenty of water.

On a long ride, frequently drinking and eating the right things (see p. 136) helps to stave off two major cycling problems: dehydration and the sudden sensation of weakness known as the 'bonk' or 'the knock'.

Unfit and over-keen cyclists may start the day feeling tired and with a rapid pulse rate. They should cycle less hard and see a doctor unless they improve.

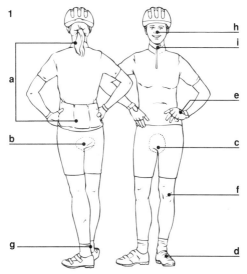

4. Cycling for fitness

HOW CYCLING HELPS

Getting and staying fit gives zest to being alive. Being fit makes you better at tackling mental and physical challenges, and less liable to fatigue, nervous tension and illness. Also, functional abilities (**1**) decline with age more slowly in a fit person (**a**) than in an unfit individual (**b**).

Regular cycling is one of the best routes to fitness. Here we show marks out of 10 given to cycling and six other activities for (**2**) aerobic (heart–lung system) fitness, the key component, and (**3**) weight control. Cycling is easier to slot into the daily routine than most other aerobic exercises. It is also kinder to knees and ankles than jogging.

1

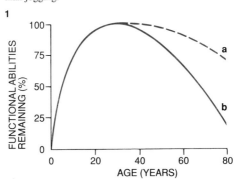

For people in normal health, a brisk cycle ride several times a week may also help to prevent the development of certain life-threatening conditions. One study suggests that a 35-year-old cyclist riding about 100km (62mi) a week reduces the risk of a heart attack by 20 per cent. Indeed, regular cycling has been shown to extend active life and increase overall lifespan. The fact that Dutch men tend to live a year and a half longer than British men might reflect the fact that between a quarter and a half of all trips are by bike in the Netherlands, against only 2 to 3 per cent in the UK. Even more significantly, research among 35- to 84-year-old former students of Harvard University suggests that cycling 60 miles a week from the age of 35 increases life expectancy by two and a half years.

2 Aerobic fitness   **3 Weight control**

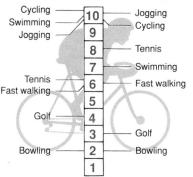

2 Aerobic fitness		3 Weight control
Cycling	10	Jogging
Swimming		Cycling
Jogging	9	
	8	Tennis
	7	Swimming
Tennis	6	Fast walking
Fast walking		
	5	
Golf	4	
	3	Golf
Bowling	2	Bowling
	1	

THE HUMAN ENGINE: HEART–LUNG SYSTEM

The main key to fitness is the heart–lung or
cardiorespiratory system (**1**). Lungs (**a**) breathe in
oxygen. The heart (**b**) pumps oxygen and digested
nutrients from food through blood vessels to muscles
(**c**). Here the sugar glucose 'burns' with oxygen to
produce muscle energy. This is the aerobic ('with
oxygen') route to energy production. In sprint cycling
(**2**), oxygen demand (**a**) outstrips supply (**b**). For a
minute or two (**c**) muscles work anaerobically ('without
oxygen'). But accumulating chemical wastes cause
oxygen debt (**d**), producing muscle fatigue. After a
minute or two you must pant and slow down to recover
(**e**) as the breathed-in oxygen removes the accumulated
wastes. Aerobic exercise yields energy more efficiently
and you can keep it up for hours.

Vigorous cycling increases the body's oxygen needs,
making the lungs and heart work harder to raise the

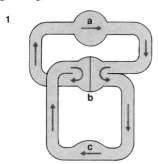

muscles' energy output. At first, sedentary people cope poorly with this increased demand. They suffer thumping hearts, shortness of breath and aching muscles. Their unexercised heart–lung systems simply cannot replace used oxygen fast enough.

If you start in reasonable health, regular cycling at over 15kph (10mph) boosts cardiorespiratory output. Lungs increase oxygen intake. The heart's pumping capacity improves. Extra capillaries form: the tiny blood vessels that supply food and oxygen to active tissues. Cycling muscles strengthen and suffer less from fatigue. Exercise burns up surplus fat in the body, checks the growth of fatty deposits in blood vessels, and helps keep their walls supple, reducing the risk of strokes and heart attacks.

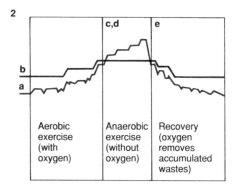

2

c,d

e

b

a

| Aerobic exercise (with oxygen) | Anaerobic exercise (without oxygen) | Recovery (oxygen removes accumulated wastes) |

THE HUMAN ENGINE: MUSCLES

When you cycle, your lower limbs act as levers, operated by skeletal muscles contracting to pull on the bones of hips, thighs, legs and feet. Skeletal muscles comprise bundles of two types of elastic fibres: red and white. Red or 'slow-twitch' fibres store plenty of oxygen, and are good at aerobic endurance work, but they react more slowly than white or 'fast-twitch' fibres. These store less oxygen, but react fast in a sprint, then soon tire. The best sprint cyclists are born with more white fibres than red, though training can improve the performance of both.

Swinging a leg to and fro as you walk uses opposed pairs of muscles: one of each pair contracting while the

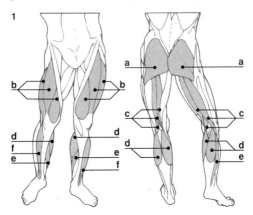

other relaxes, then vice versa. When pedalling, most of the muscular work is one-way, extending the leg. The muscle groups (**1**) that perform most of this work are (**a**) the buttock muscle (gluteus maximus), (**b**) quadriceps (a four-part frontal thigh muscle), (**c**) hamstring muscles at the back of the thigh, and (**d**) the gastrocnemius and (**e**) soleus (calf muscles). Cyclists with toe-clips or shoe cleats also use (**f**) the tibialis anterior at the front of the lower leg. Cycling tends to make leg muscles stronger and larger, but does not develop muscles of the arms, chest and back.

Stronger muscles help to improve power output. Our diagram (**2**) compares useful power output and speed of an untrained rider (**a**), touring cyclist (**b**) and sprint cyclist (**c**). The first two can ride for hours; the sprinter can ride flat out for only a minute.

2 Generated power

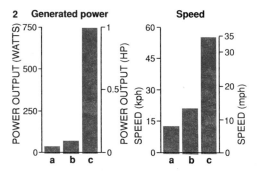

FOOD FUELS

Cyclists convert a quarter of the chemical energy in
food into mechanical motion. Most of the rest is turned
into heat. The harder you pedal, the more heat–energy
units, calories, your body consumes. Diagram (**1**)
shows the calories consumed for different levels of
activity. A long-distance cyclist uses up 8400 calories a
day, over three and a half times as much as a sedentary
person.

1

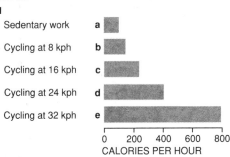

Protein-rich foods like meat, fish, eggs, milk and
cheese (**2**) build and mend tissues. The carbohydrates
(sugars or starches) in bread, pasta, potatoes, rice, fruits
and refined sugar (**3**) provide energy. Fat in cheese, ice
cream, chocolate or fatty meat (**4**) is concentrated
energy. Tiny amounts of vitamins and minerals are
vital, but they readily occur in a normal, balanced diet.
Fibre from bran, fruits and vegetables keeps the
digestive system working properly.

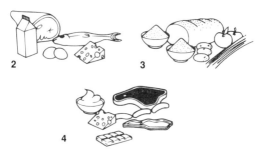

All are essential, but should not necessarily eaten as you ride. Fats and proteins take time to digest. The best energy foods are carbohydrates. These supply the blood with the sugar called glucose, an immediate energy source for muscles. Surplus glucose is stored as glycogen in the liver and muscles. Fruits and sweet drinks quickly boost your blood-sugar level, yet too much at once has the reverse effect. Breakfast an hour before starting, maybe taking a sweet drink to wash down rice, white bread, potatoes or pasta. The starch in these foods breaks down to glucose at a rate that replenishes blood-sugar levels without overloading. Have a light lunch (bread with a little meat). Save your main meal for the end of the day. Meanwhile, as you ride, snack on fruit and biscuits. Drink water often to replace the up to 2.4 litres (5 pints) per hour lost as sweat in hot weather, and maybe include a sweetened drink later on. Alcohol dehydrates, so avoid it.

IMPROVING PERFORMANCE

Before starting a cycling programme have a medical
check, a resting electrocardiogram if you are over 30
years of age, also a stress test if you are over 35 and if
heart disease, high blood pressure or diabetes run in the
family, or if you smoke heavily. Danger signs include
harsh chest pains, dizziness, lightheadedness, nausea,
breathlessness on slight exertion, or a pulse rate (**1**) of
100 or more per minute persisting 10 minutes after
exercise stops.

1

If all is well, start cycling five days a week as part of a
12-week beginner's programme, perhaps with 12-week
intermediate and advanced level sequels. Start with low
mileages and gears, and shift down on hills. Maintain a
high pedalling rate (say 80 revolutions a minute) for
increased efficiency and reduced wear and tear on
muscles and knees. (**2**) Beginners (**a**), intermediate
cyclists (**b**) and advanced cyclists (**c**) all improve as
they build up weekly cycling time: increasing speed (**3**)
and the weekly distance travelled (**4**). By intermediate
level warm up and then ride briskly for 20 to 30
minutes, with two one-minute interval sprints.
Conditioning starts at 65 per cent of maximum pulse

rate, which is about 215 minus your age. Advanced cyclists can include up to five two-minute sprints, but be sure to keep below your safe maximum pulse rate. This programme produces a training effect, improving the function of heart, lungs and muscles. After several months you may feel strong enough to tackle your first 160km (100mi) marathon.

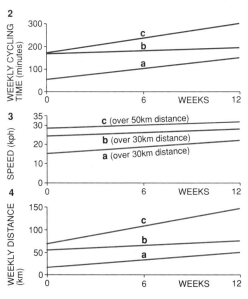

WARM-WEATHER CLOTHING

In warm weather (about 21°C and above) suitable cycling gear is lightweight and made of material that drains away sweat. Listed here are essentials and a few extras.

1 Peaked cotton cap to keep the sun off your head.

2 Towelling headband, to prevent sweat running down your forehead into your eyes.

3 Sunglasses to protect eyes from glare.

4 Short-sleeved cycling jersey with rear pocket. T-shirts and sweatshirts are other options, but all should be long enough to cover the lower back when you ride crouched forward. In changeable weather, a knitted jersey is warmer than a T-shirt. Natural fibres absorb sweat better than some synthetic materials, but cotton, except in very hot weather, may become clammy. Cotton polyester mixtures commonly feature in cyclists' jerseys and sweatshirts. Choose pale colours as they keep you cool by reflecting the sun's heat.

5 Lycra skin shorts fit snugly without pinching. Many have a chamois or synthetic lining which helps to prevent the chafing that can cause saddle soreness. Cycling shorts are worn without underwear because it also chafes.

6 Mitts with padded palms to dampen vibration and protect the hands against grazing if you fall.

7 Ankle socks of cotton, wool or wool/lycra.

8 Cycling shoes you can walk in have thinner, more flexible soles and higher heels than racing shoes.

COLD-WEATHER CLOTHING

Below 20°C you should cover your legs. The upper
body's basic need is for a windproof garment worn over
a thermal layer. In very cold weather, your upper body
may need three or more layers of clothing. If cycling
then warms you up, you can always peel off one or two
layers. Thermal protection for head, hands and feet is
also important. Apart from the items mentioned below,
one cold-weather option is a thermal T-shirt and long
johns, worn under a cyclist's tracksuit.

1 A woollen training cap has flaps to protect the neck
and ears against cold.

2 A woollen scarf can be quickly removed.

In very cold weather, you need a vest made of quick-
drying fabric, worn beneath a long-sleeved thermal
cycling jersey, with a windproof cycling jacket (**3**) as
the outer layer. A costly porous material like Gore-Tex
keeps out wind and rain yet lets perspiration escape.
Cheaper polypropylene or wool jackets let moisture out
and their nylon fronts protect against wind and rain.

4 Lycra tights keep legs warm above 10°C; for lower
temperatures you need thicker tights of wool or
polypropylene. If necessary, you can also get long
thermal underwear.

5 Warm, full-length thermal gloves protect the fingers
against chilling.

6 Thermal socks protect the feet against chilling.

7 Waterproof ankle-length boots also help to protect the
feet against cold. You can also buy overshoes.

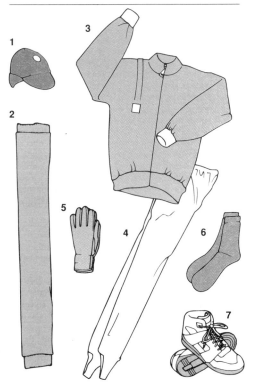

WET-WEATHER CLOTHING

Ideally, such clothing should stop rain coming in yet let
perspiration out. Impermeable rainwear could make
you as wet as if you wore none. Below we list various
options, from inexpensive but quite effective full-length
plastic capes, to expensive suits made of breathable
fabric. One or the other should keep most of your body
dry even if riding through drizzle all day. In addition, a
jacket with a waterproof front can withstand rain when
it is no more than a light shower or two.

1 A plastic cape with a built-in hood and thumb loops
should be big enough to sit on and come down over the
handlebars. Air circulating beneath helps to disperse
sweat. Capes tend to billow about in the wind, but they
can be much cheaper than rainsuits.

2 A racing cape is flimsy and light, but leaves the head
and legs exposed, and, unless made of a breathable
fabric lets the sweat condense on your body.

3 A waterproof suit made of a breathable fabric lets
perspiration out, but stops the rain getting in. Such suits
are expensive, but better than rainsuits which trap sweat
close to the body. Overtrousers need to be generously
cut to allow the knees to bend freely.

4 Overshoes or (**5**) waterproof spats keep the feet dry.
In an emergency, you can make head and arm holes in a
plastic bin liner and pull it on over your head. To keep
the head and feet dry, use a plastic shopping bag as a
hat (making sure it won't slip down over your face) and
pull two bags over your shoes, tucking them into the
tops of your socks.

TRAINING INDOORS

To keep fit, train all year round. If you miss one week, it takes several weeks to get back into shape. In winter many people are driven indoors by ice, snow or darkness. Even so, all is not lost. You can practise on a stationary cycling machine.

1 Exercise bikes These range from cheap, tinny products to sophisticated, but often uncomfortable, ergometers with a heavy flywheel to let you alter the resistance, and a computer to monitor speed, distance and calorie consumption.

2 Bicycle rollers These involve balancing as you pedal your bicycle on a set of rollers on the floor. However, rollers offer little resistance unless they have fan or magnetic resistance attachments.

3 Windtrainers, alias wind-load training devices These support your own bicycle, without its front wheel, on a stand. As you pedal, the rear wheel drives a fan, generating wind resistance which increases with the speed. Useful extras can include an electronic speedometer and a pulse-rate monitor. Magnetic trainers are quieter alternatives.

Train for half an hour to an hour. You may need a fan to cool you, and towelling to protect your handlebar stem and top tube from sweat damage. Varying the pedalling rate or resistance every few minutes helps to reduce boredom. So does listening to music or watching television. Some gymnasiums and health clubs provide a television monitor depicting a rider's progress through an imaginary landscape. A group of cyclists all watching one screen can even compete in a static road race.

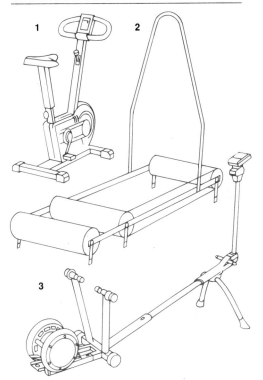

1

2

3

EXERCISES TO PREVENT STIFFNESS

Calisthenics (rhythmic, repetitious movements) and
stretching exercises (stretching muscles and joints, and
keeping them stretched for at least half a minute)
loosen joints and increase flexibility. They help you
warm up before cycling and recover after a hard ride,
preventing stiffness and even stress-induced cycling
problems. A daily session of 10 to 20 minutes is
enough. Here are four stretching (**1–4**) and four
calisthenics exercises (**5–8**).

1 Neck and shoulders Roll your head slowly around
one way, then the other. Neck and shoulder pain can
result from cycling in a fixed position. Neck rolling
helps keep neck and shoulder muscles supple.

2 Quadriceps Stand on your right leg and with your
left hand grasp your left ankle and pull it upward. After
half a minute, repeat with the other leg. Stretching the
quadriceps (frontal thigh) muscles before exercise helps
to prevent cramping.

3 Hamstrings Stand with your feet crossed and let your
head and arms flop down and forward. After half a
minute, repeat with legs crossed the other way. Do this
before and after cycling. Reducing tension in the
hamstrings may relieve lower-back pain.

4 Calves Lean against a wall, extending one foot
behind the other so as to stretch the back of the lower
leg. After half a minute, repeat, with leg positions
reversed. The benefits can include helping to prevent
stress injuring the Achilles tendon.

5 Arm swings. **6 Windmilling**. **7 Knee lifting**.
8 Leg lifting.

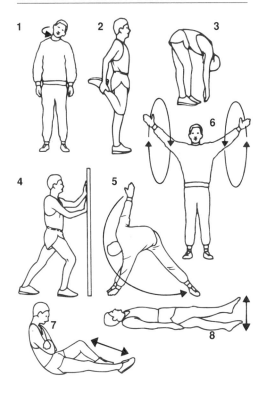

5. Touring

TOURING BICYCLES

People have accomplished long journeys on all kinds of bicycles, from penny-farthings to the heavy, single-geared army bike which nurse Dervla Murphy rode from Ireland to India in the 1960s. But most cyclists would prefer one of the types shown here. (See also p. 74.) Wide-tyred mountain bikes are designed for off-road work. Sports bikes and lightweight mountain bikes are best for fast touring, where the luggage goes on ahead.

1 Dedicated touring bike This has a sturdy load-bearing frame, a long wheelbase, long chainstays, a wide spread of gears and drop handlebars. Its fairly narrow tyres are designed for roads. (See also p. 26.)

2 Sports tourer This has drop handlebars and a wide spread of gears, but weighs less and handles more responsively than (**1**). It serves for fast touring with only light luggage.

1

2

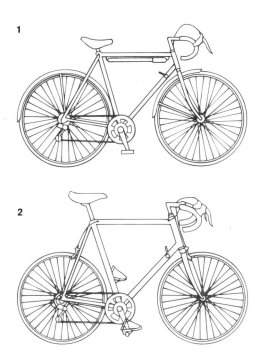

3 Sports/roadster hybrid This has a roadster's broad saddle and flat handlebars, but a lightweight frame and five or more gears. It is not the ideal bike on which to ride long daily mileages.

4 Touring mountain bike This has a sturdy load-bearing frame, knobbly tyres, straight handlebars, up to 21 gears, a long wheelbase and long chainstays. It is slower than (**1**) on smooth roads, but ideal for long rides over off-road routes with some steep gradients.

5 Lightweight mountain bike This is a light, off-road machine, with a shorter wheelbase and chainstays than (**4**). It is not designed for carrying large loads.

3

4

5

TOURING CLOTHES

For warm-weather touring (1) a cotton T-shirt or short-sleeved cyclist's jersey with back pockets is usually suitable (a). You may be glad of a lightweight, windproof, showerproof jacket on a long downhill run. Some cyclists wear long stretch-fabric cycling shorts (b), while others prefer shorts in a more loose-fitting, traditional style (c). Either type should have a seat lining and a colour that does not show dirt. The ankle socks (d) should be of thin cotton, worn with stiff-soled cycling shoes (e). Fingerless gloves (f) protect the hands from numbness and injury, and a safety helmet (g) is a sensible extra. Sunglasses (h) or a peaked cap

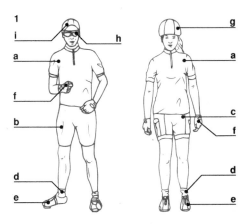

(**i**) help to reduce glare. Worn back-to-front a peaked cap guards the neck from sunburn.

For cold-weather touring (**2**) you need layers of clothing. Several thin layers are warmer than one thick layer. Begin a ride with several layers and if you warm up you can start peeling them off. Some cyclists wear a flexible but windproof and waterproof suit (**a**) as the outer layer. Long woollen stockings (**b**) are worn with cycling shoes without ventilation holes, or with overshoes (**c**). Cold-weather tourers may wear woollen gloves (**d**) over gloves of a thinner material, as well as a scarf (**e**) and a woollen ski hat (**f**), and even a balaclava helmet if it is bitterly cold. (See also pp. 140–5.)

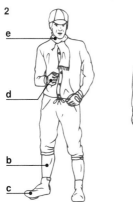
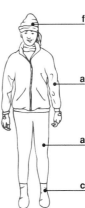

PANNIERS AND BAGS

Bicycle baggage goes in containers, which can range
from small bags holding a few tools to panniers holding
enough camping gear for a month. Materials include
lightweight, durable, waterproofed nylon and heavier,
water-repellent canvas.

Heavy loads spread between front and rear panniers
prevent the steering from becoming too light. The
higher your load, the more unstable you are, so do not
carry heavy packs on your back.

1 A handlebar bag This is handy for food, camera,
maps, etc. needed en route. A transparent map-holder
and shoulder strap for off-bike use are also useful.

2 Front panniers These are usually smaller than rear
panniers. They straddle the front wheel and are used to
spread a heavy load.

3 Rear panniers These are deep, large containers,
usually holding the bulk of the luggage. Most have rear
or side pockets and some also have a top bag. Useful
features include double zippers and carrying straps.
Rear panniers are strapped or clipped to a rack above
the rear wheel.
Other options include a pannier with shoulder straps.
This hangs from one side of a rear carrier and doubles
as a backpack. For short tours, a large saddlebag (**4**)
strapped to the saddle and seat post may be all that you
need. For a day's outing, a small bag called a seatpack
(**5**), attached like a saddlebag, will hold rainwear, tools
and valuables. Tools and wallet will fit into a framebag
(**6**), a small triangular bag strapped inside the bicycle
frame. For security, some cyclists carry valuables in a
beltbag strapped round the body.

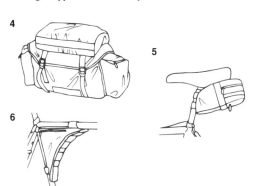

4

5

6

LUGGAGE SUPPORTS

Panniers and smaller bicycle bags need metal supports
to hold them in place, out of the way of the wheels or
other movable parts. Be sure to choose equipment
strong and rigid enough for the loads it must bear.

1 Handlebar bag carrier This may feature an uplift
support looped around the handlebars and hooked arms
that slip into sewn-on sleeves in the handlebar bag.

2 Front carrier rack This can be useful for off-road
riding as loads borne on its platform are less liable to
hit trees than panniers hung from the sides, but front-
heavy loading may impair steering.

3 Low rider frame This carries panniers on either side

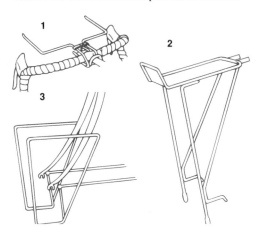

of the front wheel, to balance the rear panniers' weight without impeding steering.

4 Rear carrier rack This supports rear panniers and should be particularly rigid and strong.

5 Bungee cord This is a stretch cord with a hook at each end. It is useful for strapping bulky camping equipment on to a rear carrier rack. Some cyclists prefer to use flat straps, however.

6 Saddlebag support This sturdy, springy, slip-on metal support has ends that hook around the seat stays or are wedged between them.

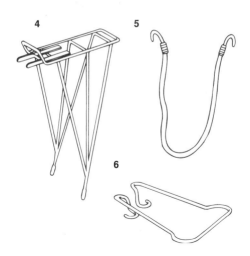

4

5

6

PLANNING A TOUR

There are cyclists who tour on impulse, with little
previous planning. But careful preparation helps you to
avoid pitfalls and make the most of your journey. Some
items are best organized several weeks or months
before you set off.

First, choose a region and route which take account of
time available, budget, preferred terrain, places of
interest and distances that you prefer to cover. Studying
maps and guide books may help you decide. Use one of
four basic touring strategies. Beginners may prefer (**1**) a
circular route with the start (**a**) and finish (**b**) in the
middle. This way you cover a lot of ground, yet remain
within easy reach of your base in case of emergency.
You could range more widely with (**2**), a circle with the
start (**a**) and finish (**b**) at the same point on its rim.
A linear route (**3**) with the same start (**a**) and finish (**b**)
would take you still further in the same time, but you
cover the same ground twice. Adventurous cyclists may
prefer (**4**), a linear route with a different start (**a**) and
finish (**b**). This requires transport to get you and your
bike to either the start or finish.

If your trip coincides with the holiday season you may
need to book travel tickets and accommodation well in
advance. Allow plenty of time for obtaining vital
documents such as passports, visas, vaccination
certificates and travel insurance.

Check your bicycle thoroughly or have it overhauled by
a bicycle mechanic.

Obtain clothing, bicycle spares and anything else you

may need, except what you can buy on the way.
Take some practice rides before you set off.

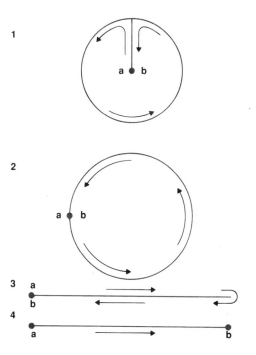

TOURING TECHNIQUES

The distance covered in a day will depend upon your experience, training and aims.

1 Reasonably fit people should easily manage 32 to 48 kilometres per day (20 to 30 miles per day).

2 Regular cyclists will go twice as far. Any further leaves too little time to stop for sightseeing, unless you ride fast.

1

32 to 48km (20 to 30mi)

2

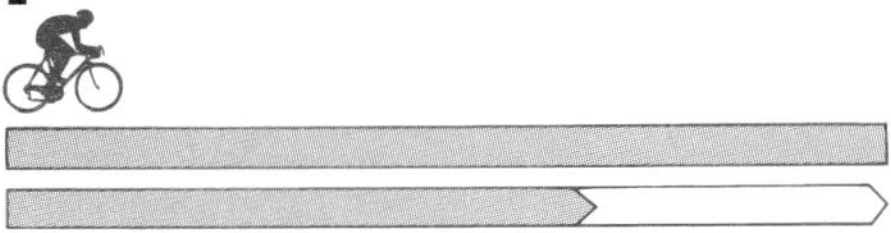

80 to 96 km (50 to 60mi)

3

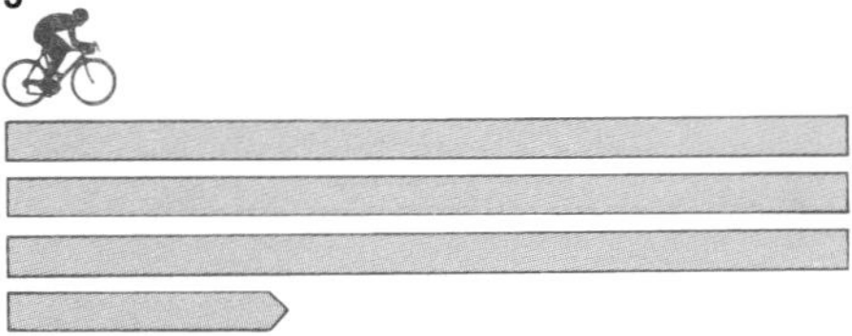

160km (100mi)

3 Super-fit enthusiasts intent only on clocking up mileage can exceed double the figure for (**2**).

Avoid busy roads and in hilly country remember that the shortest way is often the steepest; seek out well-graded roads winding up river valleys. On the flat, a rapid pedalling rate in a moderate gear can shift you along as quickly as pedalling slowly in top gear and is less tiring. On undulating ground change gears often to maintain a regular cadence (pedalling rate): aim at about 80 revolutions per minute.

Have a brief stop every hour or so. Eat and drink quite often, before you feel hungry or thirsty. On the road, avoid foods that require much digestion. A banana makes a good snack. Drink mainly water, perhaps having a sweetened drink later on, but take hot drinks if the weather is cold. Have only a light lunch and eat your main meal in the evening.

Instead of carrying heavy guidebooks, make brief notes from these in advance: on viewpoints, historic buildings, or other places worth a visit. Unless camping, also make a list of accommodation addresses and phone numbers.

Go prepared for the kinds of weather you are likely to meet (see pp. 140–5).

Each day, allow time for contingencies such as brief sightseeing stops and delays caused by a puncture, headwind, heavy shower or long hill climb.

FINDING THE WAY

To plan a long tour, use a small-scale map of a large area, for instance a scale of 1:1 000 000, where 1cm represents 10km (1 inch to approximately 16 miles). Use a map-measurer (**1**) to calculate distances, or estimate these from a specimen length printed or drawn on the map.

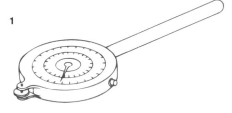

1

For day-to-day cycling, use a large-scale map giving a small area in more detail. Scales of 1:200 000, 1:100 000 and 1:50 000 show an increasing amount of detail for progressively smaller areas. Use a map (**2**) that includes major (**a**) and minor roads (**b**), and natural features such as forests (**c**) and rivers (**d**). The map should include at least spot heights (**e**) and indicate very steep hills (**f**). Hills are best shown by contour lines (**g**), which join places of the same altitude; the closer the contours, the steeper the gradient. For hilly areas, avoid road maps that give no indication of the gradients. Some weight-conscious cyclists cut up their maps, taking only the sections they need.

On the road, keep your map handy: on a map clip or
map roll attached to the handlebars for instance, or
under a transparent plastic flap on top of the handlebar
bag. For off-road riding, a compass giving your
bearings will help you to navigate.

2

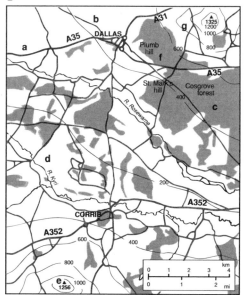

STAYING HEALTHY

Keeping fit and healthy can make the difference
between an enjoyable tour and one doomed to disaster.
Before you go, have a course of antitetanus injections.
For some foreign travel, various vaccinations are
essential. Use sun cream to prevent sunburn. In hot
weather, drink plenty of water to prevent constipation.
To avoid traveller's diarrhoea (or worse), in areas of
doubtful hygiene boil water or add purifying tablets,
and avoid cold foods you cannot peel and cooked foods
which have been left standing.

Here are two basic checklists of items essential for
keeping yourself clean and preventing or treating most
minor medical problems.

PERSONAL HYGIENE
- nail scissors
- comb
- mirror
- soap
- shampoo
- flannel
- small and large towels
- toothpaste
- toothbrush
- shaving gear
- cotton wool
- cold-water detergent

(Some items can be carried
in a sponge bag.)

MEDICAL KIT
- prescribed medicines
- spare spectacles (if worn)
- tweezers
- aspirin (or other
  painkilling tablets)
- sticking plasters
- elastic bandage
- cotton wool
- insect repellent
- insect-bite ointment
- anti-diarrhoea tablets
- sun cream

(Many items can be carried
in a medical pouch.)

PACKING

List everything you think you might need, including
bicycle tools and spares, then cross off the inessentials.
Each piece of luggage means extra pedalling effort, so
pack as little as possible. Choose the lightest items fit
for their purpose. Reduce spare tops, underclothes and
socks to one set of each. (Wash used clothes. In cool
weather, wring out, press in a towel and hang up to
dry.) For a warm-weather tour 5kg (11lb) of luggage
may be enough if you eat and sleep indoors, but at least
15kg (33lb) if you camp – more in cold weather.

Place personal items such as cash, credit cards,
identification, insurance documents and travel tickets in
secure pockets or a beltbag.

Place most other things in waterproof, plastic bags: one
each for cooking utensils, food, sleeping gear, toiletries,
first-aid kit, spare clothes, maps, and bicycle tools. Put
fluids and powders in narrow bottles. Pack seldom-
used items in the bottoms of panniers. On the top place
frequently-used items and those needed fast in an
emergency (for instance, a first-aid pack). Make full
use of each pannier bag's depth and length, so that it
does not bulge and make closing a problem. Rainwear
and bulkier items (such as a tent and sleeping pad) can
be strapped on top of your carrier. Handy items, like
sun cream, snack food, bicycle lock and the map are
best carried in a handlebar bag. If possible, fit two
water bottles on your bike frame.

TENTS AND SLEEPING BAGS

Camping can save cash and extend your cycling range.
Approved camping sites offer basic facilities and some
security. Camping 'wild' (where allowed) gets you into
more remote countryside, but cyclists should ask
landowners' permission and choose sites with care.
While camping gives extra freedom, it also adds to the
bulk and weight of your luggage, and 'wild' campers
may need extra water. However, if there are several
cyclists the load can be shared. Essential items for
camping are a tent, sleeping bag and sleeping pad.
Basic tent shapes include dome (**1**), tunnel (**2**), single
pole (**3**) and ridge (**4**). Each has its disadvantages and
advantages. Sizes range from one-person lightweights
at only 1kg (about 2lb) up to four-person tents, the
largest you can take on a bike. Double-wall tents must
have a waterproof outer skin. The best tents feature a
waterproof fabric that breathes, a waterproof floor and

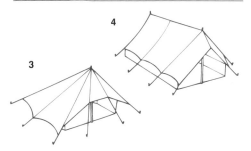

a porch for setting up the cooking gear. To erect a tent you may need aluminum tent poles, pegs and a mallet. Down-filled sleeping bags (**5**) can weigh less than 1kg (under 2lb), but cost more and once wet are harder to dry than bags filled with artificial fibre. Your bag should have a hood to help keep your head warm. A built-in or separate foam pillow is also a good idea. For improved insulation and comfort, lay your bag on a foam sleeping pad (**6**).

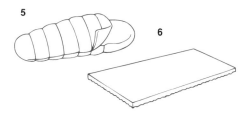

COOKING AND EATING

Self-catering campers need to take cooking equipment,
fuel, matches, food, water and kitchen utensils. Select
items that will keep the weight to a minimum.
Where there is no wood to burn or wood fires are
banned, use a camping stove that burns (1) butane gas,
(2) liquid fuel (paraffin ignited by methylated spirits),
or (3) solid fuel (alcohol tablets). The stove should burn
a fuel you can easily replenish as you go.

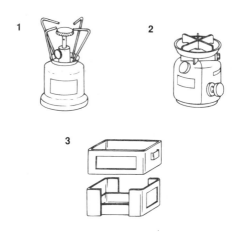

Some campers favour petrol, though careless use could make this fuel especially dangerous.

Heat food and boil water in aluminium billycans (**4**), which come in various sizes and fit readily inside each other. The lids may double as frying pans or plates.

For eating and drinking you need only (**5**) a plate, plastic mug, aluminium knife and spoon, and a combined can-opener and bottle-opener.

Wash cooking utensils in (**6**) a collapsible plastic basin filled from a foldable water container. You also need cold-water detergent and a scouring pad.

If camping wild, extinguish fires and leave no hot embers. Bury food and body waste in a hole dug in the ground. For this you need at least a trowel.

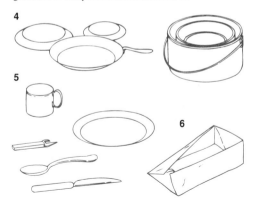

SLOPE, SPEED AND EFFORT

The steeper the slope and the heavier the cyclist or
bike, the greater the effort hill-climbing demands. Low
gears and gentle gradients reduce effort, but require
more pedalling to reach the same height.

The rate at which a cyclist's muscles apply force
to move rider and bike against gravity shows the
cyclist's muscular power, which can be measured in
horsepower (hp).

**Hill climbing in the Pyrenees
in the Tour de France**

Everyday cyclists are unlikely to want to produce more than 0.1hp. Averagely fit cyclists cannot produce more than 0.54hp for more than seven minutes.

1 If power output stays at 0.27hp, the speed drops sharply as the gradient steepens:
a 34kph (21.1mph) on the flat
b 17kph (10.6mph) on a 5% slope
c 8.5kph (5.3mph) on a 10% slope
Maintaining a speed of 20kph (12.4mph) as the gradient steepens means sharply increasing power.

1   Speed (kph) at power output of 0.27hp.

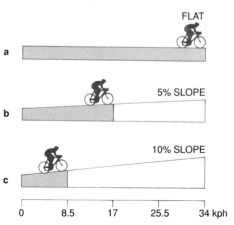

FLAT
a

5% SLOPE
b

10% SLOPE
c

0   8.5   17   25.5   34 kph

RIDING UP SLOPES

Lifting a 90.7kg (200lb) load 122m (400ft) vertically
(**1**) requires stupendous muscular strength. Cyclists
easily raise such loads (rider plus bike) to such heights
by riding up a road with a well-graded slope (**2**). With
any such inclined plane, the longer the slope in relation
to the vertical rise, the smaller the force required for
raising a load.

1

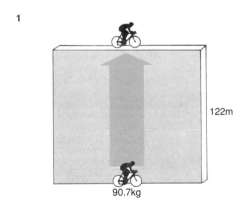

122m

90.7kg

2

RIDING DOWNHILL

Cycling uphill slows progress, but stores potential energy. Safety permitting, touring cyclists can use this for effortlessly freewheeling quickly downhill. Gravity now helps instead of hindering. Acceleration (**1**) is greater down steep slopes (**a**) than gentle slopes (**b**). Freewheeling sports cyclists can exceed 80.5kph (50mph) on long mountain descents. Touring cyclists should never risk cycling that fast, but instead pump their brakes on and off lightly to check speed without overheating the rims. Overheating might cause a tyre to burst.

1

a

b

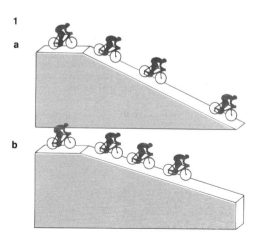

HILL TECHNIQUES

Weight hampers climbing. Lightweight cyclists and those with light loads climb faster than heavy cyclists or those with a lot of luggage. However, the latter go the fastest when freewheeling downhill. All cyclists travel faster downhill than up, but a climb and descent take longer than cycling the same distance on a level road.

Good climbing technique (**1**) helps you take hills in your stride. As you approach a hill (**a**) change down one or more gears, maintaining a fast pedalling rate. Hold the handlebars firmly; if your bike has drop handlebars, grip the drops (hooks) or brake-lever hoods and crouch forward (**b**) to prevent the front wheel lifting. Anticipate changes in the gradient, changing down as the hill steepens. At the top (**c**) reduce power to let your muscles recover. Test the brakes (**d**) before your descent. Change up as you accelerate(**e**), but rest your legs and (**f**) brake to keep your speed in control. Resume pedalling (**g**) at the foot of the hill.

1

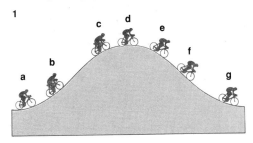

On short, steep hills 'honking' (**2**) ('dancing' out of the saddle), uses body weight to reinforce muscular effort. Gripping the handlebars firmly, (**a**) stand in the saddle, swinging the bike left beneath you as you bring your weight down on the right pedal, then (**b**) swing the bike right as you bring your weight down on the left pedal. Take care that the bike does not topple if laden with panniers. Another option on short, steep hills is 'ankling' (**3**), pivoting your feet to exert pressure on each pedal for 75 per cent of its circle.

2

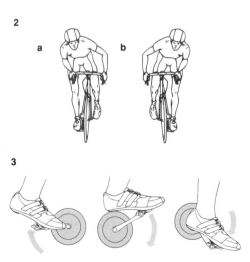

3

AGAINST THE WIND

Tailwinds speed you along, but riding into a headwind can be as tiring as slogging up a long mountain slope. Your only course is to keep your head and body low to reduce wind resistance, and peg away in low gear to avoid increasing effort to the point of exhaustion.

In strong crosswinds you risk being blown against passing traffic. If you can, use roads where trees or hedges shield you against the wind's full force. Otherwise, grip the handlebars firmly and steer slightly into the wind, alert for sudden shifts in its strength or direction.

The faster wind blows past your body or the faster you ride, the greater the air speed and the greater its cooling effect. Wind-chill can increase dangerously if you ride fast into a cold headwind (**1**). In dry conditions a still-air temperature of 10°C effectively falls below freezing if air speed rises to 40kph (25mph) (**a**). If you, your clothing, or the air is wet, wind-chill intensifies, so that still-air at 10°C effectively falls below minus 10 at an air speed of 40kph (25mph) (**b**). In cold weather and on long mountain descents, cyclists should wear windproof clothing and protect their extremities.

Passing traffic creates wind hazards too. A long, high-sided lorry (**2**) creates a bow-wave (**a**) which pushes the cyclist aside, followed by suction (**b**) which pulls the cyclist along. While being overtaken, grip the handlebars firmly to hold a straight course.

1

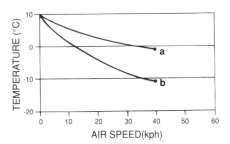

2

IN SUN AND RAIN

Hot weather brings risks of dehydration, sunburn and
perhaps even heatstroke. Drink extra water. Apply a sun
cream and wear a peaked cap and sunglasses to reduce
glare. Riders with sensitive skin may also put on a
long-sleeved shirt. In very hot weather, try to do most
of your cycling before the day's heat grows intense or
after it fades. In some countries in summer, even late
afternoon can be roasting because the road surface is
still radiating heat which it absorbed hours earlier.

Rain poses different problems, especially cold rain
which can chill your body. Put on suitable rainwear (see
p. 144) and make sure your luggage is stowed in
waterproof plastic bags. Then slog it out. Riding
through rain feels less tiresome than it looks, provided
your body is well waterproofed and your bike has
mudguards to stop surface water splashing up over your
legs. If spray thrown up by traffic forces you close to
the side of the road, look out for puddle-filled potholes.
Also beware oily road surfaces made slippery by rain
after a period of dry weather. Remember that bicycle
brakes are far less effective when wet.

Cover as much ground as you can in one or two long
spells of riding. In cold, chilling rain, though, stopping
more often for a hot drink helps maintain the body's
core temperature and prevent hypothermia.

In fog use your lights and keep close to the side of
the road.

WHERE TO GO

1 Europe This offers a wide choice of scenery and climate. Lowlands with large river valleys stretch from southern England to Russia. Mountains occur in much of north, south and south-central Europe. The most popular touring areas include picturesque parts of the British Isles (**a**), France (**b**), the Netherlands (**c**), Austria (**d**), Germany (**e**), and Denmark (**f**). Bikeways cover much of the Netherlands, and by 2000 one should almost span the length of the UK, while rural France and Germany already abound in quiet, well-surfaced

1

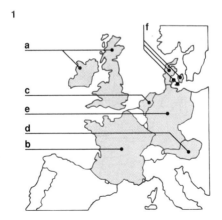

roads. Summer is the warmest season and is hot and dry in the south. Spring and autumn can be delightful, but most cyclists find European winters too cold or wet for enjoyment. High mountains are often chilly or cool and Atlantic coasts rainy.

2 North America Lowland Ontario, scenic New England and the Rocky and Sierra Mountains are favourite cycling areas, and Bicycle USA's *Almanac* provides much useful cycle touring information for each state in the US. Major cycling routes include the California Aqueduct Bikeway and Ohio Bikeway, while the Trans-America Bike Trail's two routes (**a, b**) cross the US from west to east.

2

Australasia Cyclists tend to stay near the populous parts of Australia's coastland. Inland lie vast, inhospitable deserts. New Zealand offers diverse scenery and a more temperate climate.

Other continents Much of Africa, Asia, and Central and South America is best left to experienced, self-reliant cyclists. Besides fine sights and hospitable people, some of the countries have harsh terrain and climates, debilitating diseases, lawlessness, corrupt border officials and civil wars. Cyclists should avoid places where they could be imprisoned or worse.

ORGANIZED TOURS

Taking an organized cycling holiday can be a good way to start cycle touring. Some firms offer comprehensive deals which include transport to and from the holiday area, pre-researched routes, maps, pre-booked accommodation, purpose-built cycles, repair kits, panniers, maybe a van to transport luggage and spare bikes, instruction on simple repairs and help if your bike breaks down. There are tours with a group leader, and tours where you ride independently, choosing your own route and meeting the rest of your group only at the end of the day, or else finding your own camp site, guesthouse, hostel or hotel. The leisure sections of national newspapers advertise organized cycling holidays. These may cost more than going alone, but they relieve you of trouble and worry.

TRANSPORTING A BICYCLE

You may may need to transport your bicycle by car,
bus, train, plane or ship to reach the starting or finishing
point of your tour. As for public transport, enquire
beforehand about conditions and cost (bikes
may go free).

By car There are several ways of taking a bicycle by
car: inside, with the wheels removed, or on a roof-
mounted carrier (**1**), or hung from a rear-end carrier (**2**).
Some carriers take up to five machines. Make sure the
carrier is firmly attached to the car and the bikes
to the carrier.

By bus Many buses can take bicycles in luggage
compartments, but protect them against damage.

By train Bicycles should be labelled, placed in the

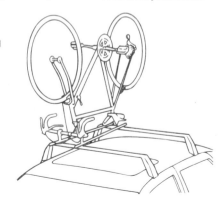

1

baggage van, lashed upright by elastic cord to a rigid
support, and left locked. Remove panniers and pump.
By air Some airlines specify dismantling and packing
in a bicycle box made of fibreglass, fabric or cardboard.
Even so, a number accept machines just with the
handlebars turned sideways, pedals reversed or
removed and tyres half deflated. For protection,
cautious cyclists should remove the rear derailleur and
cushion the frame and chainwheel with cardboard or
bubble plastic. To avoid a baggage surcharge, keep the
weight of checked-in luggage, including the bicycle,
below 20kg (44lb).
By ship On roll-on-roll-off ferries you simply cycle
aboard and lash your machine to a rail at the side of the
vehicle deck. Use your own elasticated straps or cords,
not an oily ship's rope which may be all that is on offer.

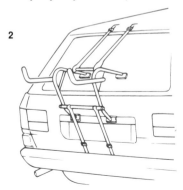

2

USEFUL TERMS ABROAD
Even if you cannot speak a foreign language fluently,
knowing the foreign words for key bicycle terms may
help you to obtain repairs or replacements.

English	French	German
battery	la pile	die Batterie
bicycle	la bicyclette, le vélo	das Fahrrad
bolt	le boulon	der Bolzen
brakes	les freins	die Bremsen
cable	le câble	das Kabel
chain	la chaîne	die Kette
dynamo	la dynamo	der Dynamo
fork	la fourche	die Vordergabel
gears	les vitesses	die Gänge
handlebars	le guidon	der Lenker
inner tube	la chambre à air	der Schlauch
light	le feu	das Licht
lock	l'anti-vol	das Schloß
loosen, to	desserrer	losschrauben

Dutch	Spanish	Italian
de batterij	la pila	la pila
de fiets	la bicicleta	la bicicletta
de bout	el tornillo	il bullone
de remmen	los frenos	i freni
de kabel	el cable	il cavo
de ketting	la cadena	la catena
de dynamo	el dinamo	la dinamo
de voorvork	la horquilla	la forcella
de versnellingen	los cambios	la marce
het stuur	el manillar	il manubrio
de binnenband	la cámara de aire	la camera d'aria
het licht	el faro	la luce
het slot	el seguro	il lucchetto
losmaken	destornillar	svitare

English	French	German
nut	l'écrou	die Mutter
oil	l'huile	das Öl
pedal	la pédale	das Pedal
pump	la pompe	die Pumpe
puncture	la crevaison	die Reifenpanne
repair, to	réparer	reparieren
saddle	la selle	der Sattel
screwdriver	le tournevis	der Schrauben-zieher
spanner	la clé anglaise	der Schlüssel
spoke	le rayon	die Speiche
sprocket	le pignon	das kettenrad
tighten, to	resserrer	anziehen
tyre	le pneu	der Reifen
valve	la valve	das Ventil
wheel	la roue	das Rad

Dutch	Spanish	Italian
de moer	la tuerca	il dado
de olie	el aceite	l'olio
het pedaal	el pedal	il pedale
de pomp	la bomba	la pompa
de lekke band	el pinchazo	la foratura
repareren	reparar	riparare
de zadel	el sillín	la sella
de schroeve-draaier	el destornillador	il cacciavite
de moersleutel	la llave inglesa	la chiave inglese
de spaak	el radio	il raggio
de kettingwiel	el piñón	il pignone
aandraaien	apretar	stringere
de buitenband	la llanta	il pneuma-tico
het ventiel	la válvula	la valvola
het wiel	la rueda	la ruota

GREAT BICYCLE JOURNEYS

Most touring cyclists travel a few hundred kilometres in a week or two. A few dedicated tourers cover thousands of kilometres on expeditions lasting months or even years. Here we list a few famous rides and riders.

1 H. Blackwell and **C.A. Harman** (UK): first to ride from Land's End to John o'Groat's (the length of Great Britain), 1880. They rode ordinaries (penny-farthings).

2 Thomas Stevens (USA): first to ride across the United States, April to August 1884, and first around the world, 1884–7; distance actually cycled about 21 700km (13 500mi). Stevens rode an ordinary.

Walter Stolle (Czechoslovakia/UK): his longest tour was about 644 000km (400 000mi), 1959–76, and he travelled through 159 countries.

1

Nicholas and **Richard Crane** (UK): first ride to 'the centre of the Earth', the place (in northwest China) furthest from the sea – 5332km (3313mi), 1986. **Bret Anderson**, **Daniel Buettner**, **Martin Engel** and **Anne Knabe** (USA): first to ride the length of the Americas (Alaska to Chile) – about 24 570km (15 267mi), 1986–7. **Annie Londonberry:** first woman to tour the world solo by bicycle in the 1890s. **Anne Mustoe** (UK): first woman to ride solo around the world, following historic trade and military routes, 1987–8; distance actually cycled 18 591km (11 552mi). In 1993, she marked her 60th birthday by starting a second world tour in the reverse (east–west) direction.

6. Racing

THE RACING CYCLIST

The 'typical' racing cyclist is 1.75m (5ft 9in) tall (about average height), weighs 68.58kg (151.2lb), and has less body fat than almost any other athlete. Our diagrams show how the racing cyclist's physique (**4**) compares to basic human body types, where (**1**) is fat and stocky, (**2**) is muscular and (**3**) is tall and thin. Among Olympic athletes, cyclists come close to the average, being less muscular than boxers or gymnasts, but more muscular than jumpers or long-distance runners. There are some differences in the physiques of different types of racing

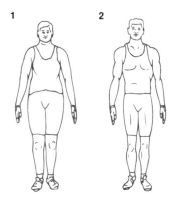

1   **2**

cyclist, though. Sprinters tend to be shorter and more heavily built than hill climbers, whose muscular but lean and lightweight bodies are an advantage when riding against gravity. Top road racers have a body form between these two. Of course there are exceptions: for example, unusually tall and powerfully built riders have won the formidable Tour de France. Age-graded competitions for both sexes mean that racing cyclists can be as young as 8 or older than 65. Although performance tends to peak in the 20s, Eddy Merckx became world amateur road-racing champion at 19, while Reg Harris won a major sprint championship in his mid-50s.

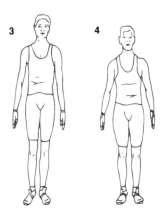

RACING GEAR

What you wear depends partly on the type of race, racing regulations and weather (see pp. 140–145). Triathletes (**1**) wear what they please. Time triallists (**3**) favour smooth, wrinkle-free skinsuits and streamlined, teardrop-shaped helmets. Road-racing cyclists (**2**) wear a synthetic or woollen jersey or shirt with a front zipper and pockets in the back for food, tools or an extra water bottle. (Track racers' jerseys may be thinner and pocketless.) Long, close-fitting, synthetic shorts go next to the skin. A soft lining sewn into the seat prevents chafing and soaks up sweat. Leather gloves with cut-off fingers and padded palms prevent numbness and

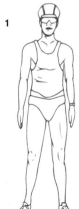

1

2

protect the hands in a fall. Socks are of seamless cotton
or wool. The stiff-soled cycling shoes have plates
called cleats which lock onto the pedals. Items
specified in racing regulations include safety helmets.
Contestants preferring to ride bare-headed in hot
weather may incur fines. A peaked cap and lightweight
racing cape may be a racing cyclist's only concession to
rain. A newspaper shoved down inside the jersey before
starting a fast, cold, mountain descent guards against
chilling.

Most racing cyclists shave their legs. Smooth legs
increase speed only a fraction, but they are easier to
clean if cut or scratched in accidents.

3

TRAINING

Training for racing involves improving strength, speed, stamina and such riding techniques as prolonged pedalling at 120 revolutions per minute. Riders practise long rides and short sprints. Endurance training involves nonstop rides of at least 100km (about 60mi) at a high cruising speed. This is aerobic work, where breathing keeps pace with the muscles' oxygen needs. Sprinting involves a flat-out dash for 10–50 seconds. This is anaerobic work, as the body runs into oxygen debt and the rider must slow down to let heart rate and breathing subside. In ladder sprinting (**1**) riders step up sprint distance (**a**) and recovery distance (**b**), using lamp-posts or telegraph poles as markers. Experienced riders inject 10-second sprints and 10-minute periods at high speed into a long ride to simulate racing conditions. Between them, endurance riding and sprinting strengthen muscles, and improve oxygen uptake and the heart's blood-pumping capacity. But experts warn that sprinting may impair the hearts of beginners and under 17s.

1

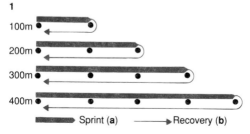

100m

200m

300m

400m

▬▬▬ Sprint (**a**)   ⟶ Recovery (**b**)

Some racing cyclists plan their year (**2**) with overlapping schedules of road training (**a**), circuit training (**b**) or training on indoor ergometers or windload simulators, road racing (**c**), off-road racing (**d**), stretching and other exercises (**e**), weight training (**f**), and running or swimming (**g**). Competitive riding demands at least three cycle training sessions a week. A week's practice lost takes three weeks to recover.

2 **a** Road training   **e** Stretching exercises
    b Circuit training **f** Weight training
    c Road racing   **g** Running or swimming
    d Off-road racing

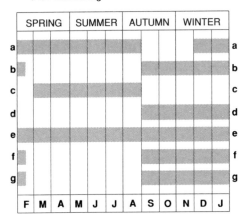

ROAD RACES

Single-day road races and stage road races (races
spread over several days) include mass-start events for
professionals and amateurs. The world's most famous,
and toughest annual stage race is the Tour de France. It
lasts about 20 days in July and covers more than
3220km (2200mi) on roads temporarily closed to all
other traffic. Our map shows one year's route (1992)
with three individual time trials (stages 1, 9, 19) and
one team time trial (stage 4). The route varies from year
to year. Sometimes some stages take place outside
France, but the hardest days always involve severe
mountain climbs in the Alps and Pyrenees. Speeds can
average 40kph (25mph) on the flat and reach 64 kph
(40mph) in sprint finishes, and more than 80kph
(50mph) on mountain descents.

One hundred and eighty professional cyclists take part
in the Tour, though many drop out through illness,
injury or exhaustion. The riders are grouped in 20 trade
teams. Each team may include specialist time triallists,
hill climbers and sprinters. Most team members are
workers (*domestiques*) whose main task is supporting
their team's strongest all-round cyclist. During the race
the overall leader wears a yellow jersey, the leading
sprinter a green jersey, and the leading climber a white
jersey with red polka dots. The Tour winner is the rider
awarded the shortest overall time, and there are special
awards for the king of the mountains (the rider who
scores the most points on designated hill climbs) and
the top point-scoring sprinter.

Tour De France (1992)

- ● Start (San Sebastián)
- • Town (stage start or finish)
- ◉ Town (Dole; rest day)
- ⬤ Individual time trial
- ⬤ Team time trial
- ● Finish (Paris)

→ Route
⇢ Transfer

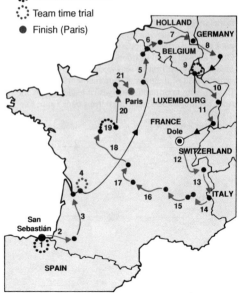

ROAD-RACING TECHNIQUES

In a typical team-based road race, most riders stay in a
closely bunched pack or *peloton*. Each worker helps to
escort the team leader, and must be prepared to give the
leader his or her bike if the leader's machine suffers a
puncture or some other breakdown.

Every team tries to keep its leader near the front of the
pack, well placed to avoid pile-ups and poised to chase
riders making a sudden breakaway. If the team leader
makes a break, the workers may stay at the front of the
pack to slow down the pursuit.

Often a small group of riders from different teams
breaks away. At first all may cooperate to keep the
group ahead of the pack. Group members ride in single
file (**1**), with continuous changes of leadership as the
rider in front swings aside and drops back (**a, b, c**).

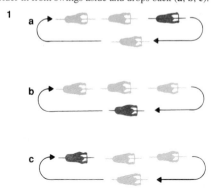

Called bit-and-bit or pace-line riding, this technique means that each rider closely follows another for most of the time. Up to 90 per cent of a solo cyclist's effort goes into combating wind resistance, but its effect is reduced by drafting behind another cyclist. Thus bit-and-bit lets the whole group ride very fast for less effort than a solo cyclist would need.

In a crosswind, a pace-line may slant across the road in echelon formation (2). Each rider, except the temporary leader, is partly shielded from the wind by the rider slightly ahead and to windward. Echelons reduce the effort needed to overcome crosswinds.

Late in a stage the pace quickens. The leading group may break up as its individuals sprint to the finish. The winner is often a rider who drafts behind the sprint leader, then overtakes just before the finishing line.

2

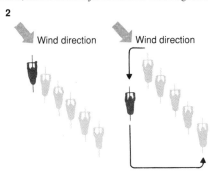

Wind direction   Wind direction

ROAD-RACING BIKES

Top-class road-racing cyclists use bicycles made of
only the finest components. The best bikes can cost as
much as a small car, and one rider may use several
during a stage race. Support vehicles carry spare
bicycles in case competitors damage their own. Also
riders may switch from one type of bike to another
from day to day to suit the terrain and type of racing.

1 Standard road-racing bicycle Riders traditionally
rely on machines with a lightweight but sturdy steel
alloy frame and well-tried high-grade components.
These bikes may weigh about 10kg (22lb).

2 Super lightweight road-racing bicycle Since 1980
road racers have turned increasingly first to aluminium
then to even lighter carbon-fibre frames to gain crucial
reductions in weight. A racing bike with a carbon fibre
frame (**a**) and metal lugs (**b**) can weigh 450g (1lb) less
than a steel alloy machine, saving vital muscular energy
on a long mountain climb (although whatever machine
a cyclist rides, the team mechanic will modify the gears
to suit the day's gradients). By the 1990s, carbon fibre

1

frames were winning major road races.

3 Time-trial bicycle This is the type of machine described on p. 207, with variations. The small front wheel (**a**) may have three large composite spokes or many metal spokes radially (not crossover) laced to trim their length and weight. Road racers switch to time-trial bikes for the few days of individual and team time trials which can decide the Tour de France.

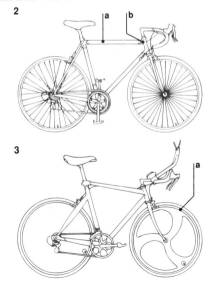

CRITERIUM RACES

Criterium races are mass-start events where riders may lap a short course 100 times or more at high speed. Cyclists may be riding as individuals or members of teams. The total race distance is usually between 40km (25mi) and 100km (62mi). Many courses involve city streets or parks, and criterium or 'round-the-houses' races are popular spectator sports, especially in the United States. Cyclists win prizes called primes for winning special laps. In one type of criterium, the overall winner is the rider with the most points for winning special laps. In another version, the winner is the first over the line.

A criterium course has many sharp bends, so this kind

1

of racing demands high-speed steering and cornering skills (**1**) as riders slow down into a bend then accelerate out of it. As in long-distance road races, the best and safest position is close to the front of the pack. A rider who falls in the middle, while jostling for position, could well bring down all those close behind. Any strongly built racing bicycle can take part in these races provided it handles responsively. The ideal criterium bike (**2**) has a stiff, short frame with a high bottom bracket (**a**) and short cranks (**b**) to allow pedalling while cornering, stiff wheels (**c**) with highly tensioned spokes and fully inflated, strongly glued tyres, a high saddle (**d**), low stem and handlebars (**e**), and bar-end gear-shift levers (**f**).

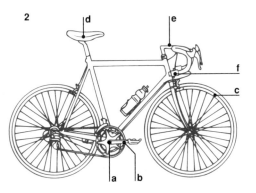

TIME TRIALS

A time trial is an unpaced road or track race against the clock. Riders, individually, cover a set distance of 16 to 160km (10 to 100 mi), or cycle for a fixed time of 1 to 24 hours. Before the race, contestants take a short ride to warm up. On the start ramp a race official stabilizes each cyclist waiting to go (**1**). Riders set off at one-minute intervals, with the fastest last. Each sets off in a low gear, accelerating and changing up rapidly to settle into a high gear, using a fast cadence (pedalling rate) of about 90 revolutions per minute. The aim is to accelerate swiftly, maintain a steady high speed and, on out-and-back courses, to achieve a quick turn-around. In one hour, the world's top time triallists can ride more than 50km (31mi).

1

Time trialling is one of the toughest of all types of cycle racing. Rules forbid drafting, so each rider must battle against wind resistance all the way. A cyclist can reduce the resulting drag factor 25 per cent by riding hunched forward on aerodynamically designed time-trial bikes. Such a bike (**2**) may have a narrow-tyred rear wheel (**a**) with a solid disc (not spokes) to reduce drag, a small front wheel (**b**), with as few as three spokes (solid front wheels get deflected by crosswinds), and only one chainwheel (**c**) to cut weight. From a steep seat tube (**d**) the top tube (**e**) slopes down, and the crouched rider grips cowhorn bars (**f**), perhaps with clip-on aero bars (**g**) for a more streamlined position.

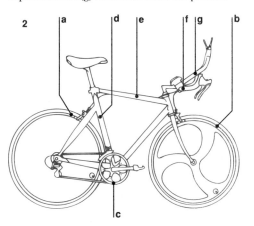

TRIATHLON

Triathlon cycling is time trialling with a difference. A triathlon tests all-round athletic ability with a long-distance swim, a cycle ride and a long-distance run, tackled one after the other. The Hawaii Ironman, the best-known and toughest one-day triathlon, involves (**1**) swimming 3.9km (2.4mi) in the sea, (**2**) cycling 180km (112mi), then (**3**) running a full marathon of 42km (26mi), all nonstop. A standard triathlon's shorter distances include a 40km (25mi) cycle ride. The strongest triathlon contestants average about 37kph (23mph), an unpaced, professional road racer's speed. Ordinary racing bikes will do, but top triathletes favour

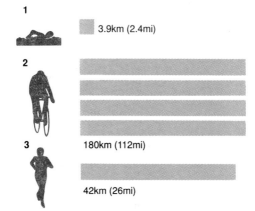

1

3.9km (2.4mi)

2

180km (112mi)

3

42km (26mi)

time-trial bikes steered only by aero-bars fitted with elbow pads on which to rest arms already fatigued by a long swim. (Calculations show that aero-bars reduce drag enough to lop three minutes off a standard triathlon.) Thumbs control gear-shift levers at the front of the bars. The triathlete bike's steep seat tube and seat post bring the saddle forward. The result is a low, streamlined riding position, with upper-body weight well distributed (**4**).

Wearing just a vest and fast-drying lightweight swimming trunks allows a triathlete to emerge from the water and get straight onto a bicycle without stopping to change.

4

OFF-ROAD RACING

There are off-road races for mountain, BMX and road-racing machines.

Off-road mountain bike races These are rugged tests of bikes and riders. Riders pedal their multigeared, fat-tyred machines up and down slopes over rough terrain, even across rocks, mud and water, using the techniques described on pp. 222–31. Besides natural hazards, mass-start cross-country events (**1**) may offer the challenge of a course too narrow for several cyclists riding abreast except at the start and finish. Courses are graded for difficulty according to age group. Senior mass-start cross-country events are among the toughest of all. One of the most famous is based in California's Mammoth Lakes mountain resort. Competitors repeat a short but arduous circuit, to clock up 58km (36mi). Off-road mountain bike contests also include hill climbs and downhill races. Mammoth Lakes features one precipitous trail where top riders average more than 64kph (40mph) as they plunge over 600m (about 2000ft) in just over 6km (about 4mi).

1

BMX track racing Helmeted children on track-racing BMX bikes race on unsurfaced tracks with hillocks and dips (**2**). A skilled rider can leap hillocks 8m (27ft) apart.

2

Cyclo-cross This provides traditional midwinter training for road-racing cyclists. Competitors ride and carry (**3**) narrow-tyred racing bikes around a course with streams, mud, or slopes as steep as a roof – sections where shouldering machines is faster than riding them.

3

OFF-ROAD RACING MOUNTAIN BIKES

This type of machine (**1**) has been called the thoroughbred of the off-road stable. Like traditional road-racing bikes, it is lightweight, comes with toe straps (**a**) and offers quick handling. Unlike road racers, of course, it has flat handlebars (**b**), extra-fat tyres (**c**) and often a wider spread of gears (**d**).

The frame materials can include steel alloy tubes 'fuse-welded' together (**e**), or aluminium tubing, with a larger diameter than steel alloy, but renowned for its stiffness and light weight. An aluminium-framed off-road racer can weigh as little as 10kg (22lb). Frame angles range from steep, for agile climbing and quick response in

1

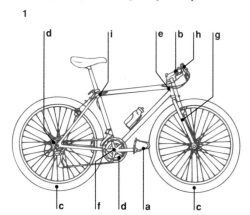

tight spots, to more gradual, for secure descents (a long wheelbase adds stability). An off-road racer's high bottom bracket (f) provides plenty of clearance for negotiating rocks, logs and mud. Other features include extra-strong straight-bladed forks (g). Gear-shift levers (h) may project above the handlebars to assist gear-changing while standing up in the saddle. Experts believe that bikes with shortened, exposed brake- and gear-cable runs (i) give improved braking and gear-changing response.

Off-road racers must be rugged enough to cope with rough trails with severe climbs (2) and descents (3).

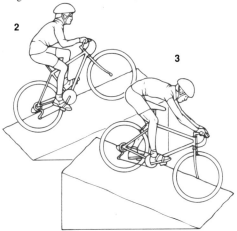

OBSERVED TRIALS

These off-road events for mountain bikes have been
likened to ballet and tightrope walking. Skill counts
more than speed. Experts are adept at wheelies, bunny-
hops and other manoeuvres described on pp. 222–33.
An observed trials ride may involve completing a
course, with 10 short but extremely difficult sections,
three times. Each section can bristle with obstacles
ranging from mud (1) and sand pits, to logs, oil drums
(2) and severe slopes. Contestants may first walk the
course, trying to plan the safest route through. On each
ride, officials add various penalty points per section for
faults such as dabbing the ground with a foot, putting
both feet on the ground, falling or hitting a marker. The
rider with the fewest penalties wins.

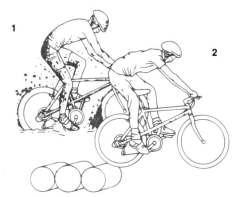

Many riders tackle observed trials on ordinary mountain bikes. Enthusiasts may favour (**3**) a purpose-built machine with a steeply angled frame (**a**); deep, reinforced forks (**b**) to withstand extra stress; high, very short chainstays (**c**) to improve 'pedal power' by reducing the distance between pedals and rear wheel; a high bottom bracket (**d**) for maximum ground clearance; a guard (**e**) shielding chainwheels against logs or other hazards; and rotary handlebar gear-shift levers (**f**) and three-finger brake levers (**g**), allowing firm handlebar grip while changing gear or braking. Ultra-specialized trials bikes have small wheels and only one (low) gear. They are useless on roads.

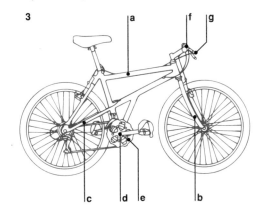

TRACK RACING

The fastest, most spectacular bicycle racing takes place in indoor and outdoor velodromes. Spectators in tiered seats look down on riders tearing around an oval track with steeply banked curves (**1**). Riders use ultra-lightweight machines without brakes or gears.

Match sprints Two (sometimes three) cyclists compete over 1000m (1070yd), but only the last 200m (219yd) are timed. Riders begin by balancing almost motionless, each trying to force the other to lead. The second cyclist can then draft, before gaining height and trying to swoop down past the leader to win, at up to 80kph (50mph).

Sprint bicycles (**2**) are cycling's 'greyhounds', weighing as little as 7kg (17lb). They have strongly-curved drop handlebars (**a**), a steep seat angle (**b**), a short wheelbase (**c**), stiffened wheels (**d**) and a fixed rear wheel (**e**), which means constant pedalling is necessary.

Pursuit races Two cyclists start at opposite sides of the track and race a set distance of up to 5km (3mi) against

1

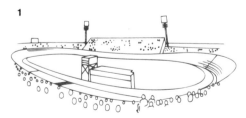

the clock and each other. The cyclist who overtakes, or records the faster time, wins. A pursuit race is often ridden between the two fastest finishers of a track time trial of 1000–5000m (1070–5468yd).

Conventional pursuit bicycles resemble road time-trial bicycles, but with a shortened wheelbase and of course no gears or brakes. However, a startlingly novel monocoque (see page 240) won the 1992 Olympic Games 4000m pursuit, and in 1993 another unorthodox bike set a new track-based, one-hour time-trial record.

Paced races Cyclists draft at around 80kph (50mph) behind motorcyclists and riders serving as windshields. One type of paced race involves a heavy motorcycle pulling a rear-mounted roller behind which the cyclist rides. His bicycle's 'reversed' front fork and small front wheel help to stabilize steering.

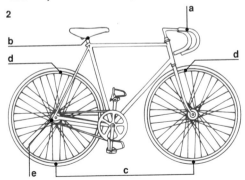

2

TRACK RACING: MASS START

Mass-start track events include points, elimination,
Madison and Keirin races. Some are entertainment
rather than serious sport.

Points racing Every fifth lap, the first five riders gain
points. The rider with the highest total wins.

Elimination (or devil take the hindmost) races At the
end of each lap (or every two or three laps) the last
rider across the finishing line drops out.

Madison races Two-man teams race. Each team's
members take turns: one rides while the other dawdles
above the banked track's stayer's line. Every few laps,
the rider gives the other a high-speed handsling (**1**)
handover. Madisons originated in the United States.
They are key features of six-day races: scaled down
versions of races in which cyclists once rode six days
almost nonstop.

1

Keirin racing This is cycling's equivalent to a dog race, in which greyhounds chase a mechanical hare around a track. At the sound of the starter's gun, nine cyclists wearing helmets and shoulder pads accelerate out of numbered stalls in pursuit of a pacemaker (**2**). Riders may not pass this 'hare', but try to secure the first place behind him. The 'hare' steps up the pace, then drops out before the last lap. The final 200m (654ft) of the 2000m (1.2mi) race is a frantic sprint and riders often collide and crash as the winner jostles to victory at more than 56kph (35mph). Keirin racing is immensely popular in Japan, where millions watch and bet on events held in more than four dozen velodromes.

2

ENDURANCE RACES

Enthusiasts claim long-distance bicycle races mark the
supreme test of stamina. We have already mentioned
the 24-hour time trial and the 180km (112mi) time trial
of the Hawaii Ironman triathlon. Here are some others.
Iditabike Competitors attempt to cross 338km (210m)
of Alaska in February. Mountain bikes with double-
width wheels help the riders to cycle and push their
way over snowy trails and icebound rivers, but the race
is called off if the weather becomes too severe (**1**).
Ultraman triathlon Inspired by the Hawaii Ironman,
this super-gruelling, two-day event involves 161km
(100mi) and 270km (168mi) rides, plus a 9.7km (6mi)
swim and finally a marathon run.

1

Race Across America In this toughest of all endurance bicycle races (**2**), competitors cross the United States from the Pacific to the Atlantic coast. The winner is the quickest to complete an almost nonstop ride of about 5000km (3100mi). The route can vary, but it may cross mountain passes up to 2750m (9000ft) high. Support vehicles provide food and mechanical aid, but the riders snatch only two to three hours' sleep a night, which reduces their average speed to about 22.5km per hour (14mph). Exhaustion or dehydration forces many to drop out. By 1990, the men's record time was down to 8 days and under 9 hours. The fastest-ever woman finisher took only about a day longer.

2

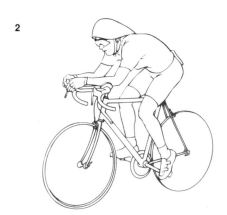

7. Cycling for fun

ROUGH RIDING

Riding over rough trails on a mountain bike allows you to explore wild countryside out of reach to everyone else except walkers. Successful off-road riding calls for special bike-handling skills if you are to negotiate mud, rocks, water and sand. Be sure to carry a toolkit for making basic repairs.

1 Deep wet mud Tackle this in bottom gear and remain seated. This is the best way of combating the high rolling resistance and helping your tyres keep their grip. Cycling through deep mud is hard work, and you need plenty of strength to keep your bike moving.

1

2 On loose, rocky ground Pedal quickly but ride
slowly in low gear. Pick your way between the biggest
rocks (**a**), pulling your front wheel up and over those
you cannot avoid (**b**).

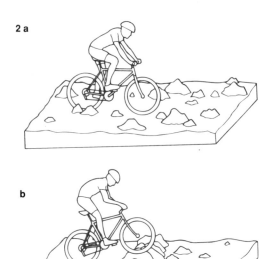

2 a

b

3 Crossing water Clear, shallow water lying on a flat firm base offers no real obstacle. To cross a rocky stream in water up to your axles, plot your route first to avoid boulders. Ride through slowly in low gear, with short, stabbing pedal strokes if deep water prevents complete pedal rotations. Beware water of unknown depth and avoid getting soaked in cold weather.

4 Dry, deep, powdery sand This clogs bicycle wheels and may force you to walk or run, carrying your bike over one shoulder (**a**). Firm, wet beach sand is easy to cycle across. Beach sand drying out at low tide falls between these conditions. Despite rear-wheel spin and slippage, slow, steady riding may get you across wet, yielding sand (**b**).

3

4 a

b

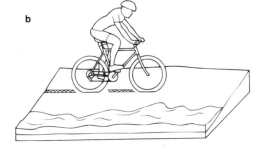

UP AND DOWN

Mountain bikers tackle steeper ascents and descents than anything a road-riding cyclist encounters. What is more, the surface is likely to be rough and loose, making the wheels tend to lose traction and slip.

1 A steep climb Before tackling a steep climb, reduce the tyre pressure to improve traction and increase power by raising the saddle for almost full leg extension. As the hill starts, get into low gear before losing momentum. Stay seated to help your rear tyre grip the surface. (Standing up in the saddle would lighten the load on the rear wheel and so increase the risk of wheelspin.) As the gradient steepens, crouch lower, keeping your weight over the bicycle. This helps to stop the front wheel lifting. All the time look ahead far enough to avoid obstacles that might make you stall or fall off.

2 A steep descent To make a long, steep descent, lower your saddle to lower the centre of gravity. Change up and sit far back, with your pedals level and knees and arms bent to reduce shock. Keeping your weight back helps the rear wheel grip and prevents it from lifting. On a very steep slope you may need to slide even further back, with your heels angled downward to help keep your behind hung out over the rear wheel. Use mainly the back brake, if necessary stabbing it on and off to prevent the rear wheel locking and skidding. Applying the front brake on a very steep slope could pitch you over the handlebars. Ride downhill slowly enough to choose a path between boulders or other obstructions.

1

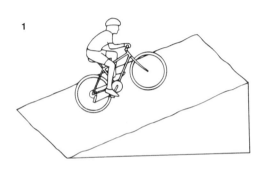

2

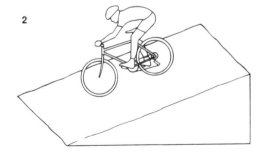

OVER THE TOP

Off-road riders can find their path blocked by an
obstacle, usually a log or a fallen branch. With
practice, you can often ride across without getting
off. Given time to assess the problem, you can probably
climb over (log hopping). You may have to clearjump
(bunny hopping) if you meet an obstacle unexpectedly
while riding fast.

1 To climb an obstacle Approach it slowly, head-on
and in low gear. As your front wheel makes contact,
pull your handlebars up (**a**), pull up on your toe-clips,
and shift your weight back over the rear wheel. As your
front wheel comes down beyond the obstacle, shift your
weight forward, rise in the saddle, and push down on
the handlebars and the pedal which is making a

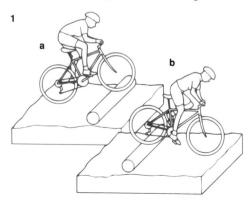

downstroke. All this pulls the rear wheel up (**b**) and over the obstacle. Before you attempt this manoeuvre be sure the obstruction is not big enough to hit and damage your big chainwheel as it travels over the top.

2 To leap over an obstacle Ride at it quickly, crouching, with arms braced. At the last moment, stand in the saddle, thrusting hands and feet downward to compress the air in the tyres (**a**). This helps to bounce the bike off the ground. Leap upward, lifting the handlebars, with your toes gripping the pedals. As the bike starts to come down, lean forward, and slightly bend knees and elbows, ready for impact (**b**). Before you attempt to cross logs this way, practise by jumping over cardboard boxes which collapse harmlessly if you hit them.

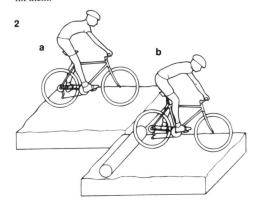

SWIVELLING

Stopping and swivelling the bike on one wheel is where
serious off-road technique might seem to give way to
stunt riding. But pivoting on the back wheel serves a
useful purpose, when you come face to face with an
obstruction too big to climb or jump over. Similarly,
pivoting on the front wheel can be a way of suddenly
altering course at a very sharp bend. Indeed, by
pivoting several times in succession, an experienced
rider reaching a dead end can turn right around almost
on the spot. Practise pivoting on soft, open and level
ground just in case you fall off.

1 To pivot on the rear wheel Stand on the pedals,
shift your weight back, use the rear brake and

yank up on the handlebars and toe-clips. As the
front wheel rises, keep braking. Hold your feet
level and grasp the handlebars, then shift your weight to
one side to turn the front of the bike in an arc. As
the wheel lands, release the brake, resume pedalling
and sit on the saddle.

2 To swivel on the front wheel Slow down, apply the
front brake and lean forward, pushing down on both
pedals. As the rear wheel rises, shift your weight to
one side to turn the back of the bike in an arc, at the
same time turn the handlebars the other way. As the
rear wheel lands, let go of the brake, resume pedalling
and sit on the saddle.

2

PERFORMING STUNTS

Mountain bikers who have mastered the skills
described so far may go on to such tricky moves as
plunging down low cliffs (known as drop-offs), and
skid-turning on rapid descents (locking the back brake
and applying a pedal to make the bike's rear end slide
around to that side). Wheelies and table topping are two
more tricky manoeuvres.

There is no need to learn any of these stunts for normal
off-road cycling. Their main purpose is simply to show
that a cyclist has magnificent control of his or
her bike. Only very accomplished mountain-bike riders
should attempt stunts and even then not on hard ground,
where falling could cause an injury.

1 To perform a wheelie A rider sits on the saddle,
left foot on the ground, right foot pressing the right
pedal down and front wheel up in the air. Balancing on

the rear wheel, the cyclist puts his or her left foot on its pedal and starts pedalling. The toe straps remain loose; indeed, some riders remove toe-clips completely. Pedalling along on the rear wheel alone calls for a supreme sense of balance.

2 To table top A rider bends both knees, rises in the saddle and bounces the bike, hauling it up much as when performing a bunny hop to jump over an obstacle. Once in the air, the rider tilts the bike sharply to one side, which lifts the lower part of the wheels, increasing the gap between ground and bike. Virtuoso riders can manage a clearance that would take them higher than a table top, but no one should try this difficult and dangerous manoeuvre until they are already expert at jumping a bicycle over an obstacle.

2

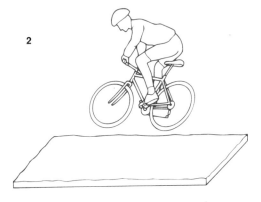

8. Perfecting the bicycle

LANDMARKS IN DEVELOPMENT

Bicycle development began in the late eighteenth century, but really took off in the 1860s. The first modern-looking bicycles appeared in the 1880s. Ball bearings, pneumatic tyres and other components invented for bikes also helped to make cars and aeroplanes possible. Most major features of bicycle design had arrived by 1906, but in the 1970s the mountain bike sparked off fresh refinements and a use of synthetic materials. Here we list the main milestones in bicycle evolution.

1791 The foot-propelled, unsteered Célérifère (**1**) developed by the Comte de Sivrac (France).

1817 The foot-propelled, steerable Draisienne or hobbyhorse (**2**) invented by Baron Karl von Drais de Sauerbrun.

1839 A steerable velocipede operated by pedals (**3**) invented by Kirkpatrick Macmillan (UK).

1861 A steerable velocipede with pedals fixed to a big front wheel (**4**) developed by Pierre Michaux (France).

1869 The world's first bicycle show, in Paris, exhibited freewheels, variable gears and contracting brakes. Ball bearings, to reduce friction, appeared at about this time.

1870 Tension wheels with radial spokes developed by James Starley (UK).

1870s Ordinaries (penny-farthings) with front wheels 1.5m (60in) in circumference (**5**).

1873 A chain drive developed by H.J. Lawson (UK).

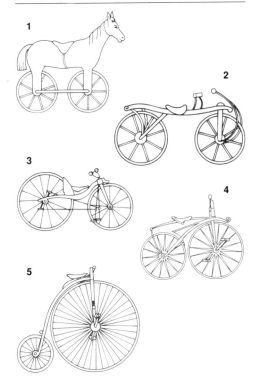

1876 Tangential spoking invented by James Starley (UK).

Late 1870s Ball bearings and tubular frames became standard.

1880 The roller bush chain (**6**) perfected by Hans Reynold (UK).

1886 The 'safety' bicycle (**7**) with wheels of equal size, direct steering, and the precursor of today's diamond frame developed by John Kemp Starley (UK).

1886 A bicycle dynamo lamp patented by Richard Weber (Germany).

1888 The pneumatic tyre (a rediscovery) patented by John Boyd Dunlop (UK).

1890 The diamond-frame bicycle design (**8**) now firmly established.

1896 A recumbent bicycle patent filed by I.F. Wales (USA).

1900 Flexible brake cables developed by Frank Bowden (UK).

1902 A three-speed hub gear produced by Henry Sturmey and James Archer (UK).

1900 The small-wheeled Bantam bicycle (**9**) was the first portable bicycle.

1906 The modern derailleur gear mechanism developed by Paul de Vivre (France).

1974 The first mountain bike (**10**) built by Gary Fisher (USA).

1974 Open-rule HPV (human-powered-vehicle) competitions stimulated new recumbent designs.

1982 The first monocoque frame (**11**) bicycle designed by Mike Burrows (UK).

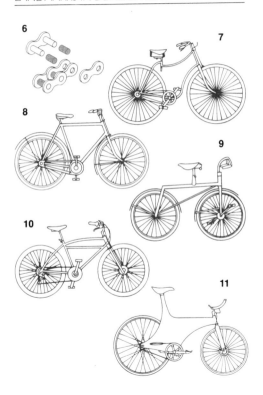

MOUNTAIN BIKES

The lively, rugged off-road mountain bike was born in
northern California in the early 1970s. The incentives
to design it were time-trials on a dirt track plunging
400m (1300ft) down Mt. Tamalpais in only 2.9km
(1.8mi). Riders called that route Repack Road because
intense braking friction burnt off their hub brakes'
lubricating grease, so they had to repack with fresh
grease after each descent.

The first mountain bikes were clumsy-looking hybrids
made of parts from various machines, and their creators
were largely amateur enthusiasts. In 1974, Gary Fisher
rescued a discarded heavy 'clunker' (**1**) with balloon
tyres (**a**), and souped it up with motorcycle brakes (**b**)

1

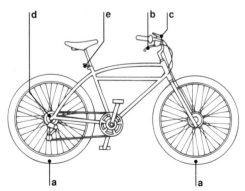

and thumb shifters (**c**), wide-range derailleur gears (**d**) and a quick-release lever (**e**) for saddle-height adjustment. Joe Breeze developed a brand-new type of frame. Erik Koski and Tom Ritchey were other innovators. In 1976, Charles Kelly commissioned the world's first purpose-built mountain bike. Commercially produced bikes appeared in 1979. Mountain bikes transformed bike sales and launched revolutions in components. By the 1990s advanced machines for road or off-road use included the Gary Fisher Procaliber (**2**) with its lightweight carbon-fibre frame (**a**), profile bars (**b**), shock absorbers (**c**) and the price tag of a motorbike.

2

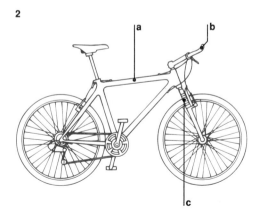

MONOCOQUES

In 1992, Britain's Chris Boardman broke the world
record for a 4000m pursuit race. His revolutionary
machine's streamlined frame reduced wind resistance
enough to give its rider 10–12 seconds' advantage over
competitors on conventional bikes.

A traditional pursuit bike (**1**) has a diamond frame (**a**)
of separate tubes, with chainstays and seat stays (**b**)
supporting the rear wheel, and a two-pronged fork (**c**)
supporting the front wheel. The new track bike (**2**) had
a streamlined monocoque frame (**a**) made of a sheet of
moulded carbon fibre built up of separate layers and
reinforced with titanium. This single-piece frame

1

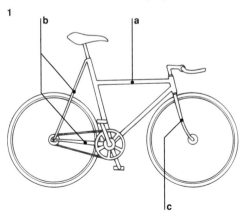

supported wheels, cranks, saddle, handlebars and a wing-shaped, one-sided 'fork' (**b**), also of carbon fibre. Other features included a carbon-fibre disc rear wheel (**c**), a three-spoked, carbon-fibre front wheel (**d**), high-performance tyres (**e**), an aluminium and titanium axle (**f**) and aerodynamically designed handlebars (**g**), pedals (**h**), chain (**i**) and sprocket (**j**). The whole machine weighed under 8.2kg (18lb).

Pioneered in 1982 by British designer Mike Burrows and developed by Lotus Cars, the monocoque marked the first big departure from diamond-frame design for a century. It might create a trend.

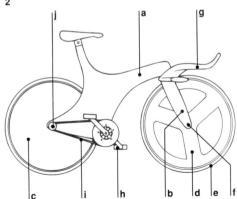

RACING RECUMBENT HPVs

The fastest bicycles and tricycles are recumbent HPVs (human-powered vehicles). As their name suggests, most have a cyclist, or cyclists, sitting or lying back, feet first; in some the cyclist is face down. The small frontal area reduces wind resistance, allowing higher speeds for less effort than with conventional bikes. At 32kph (20mph) a low-slung recumbent cuts drag by one quarter and power requirement by one-fifth. Streamlined fairings boost performance still more, producing 32kph (20mph) for half the power required by an ordinary racing bike.

Back in the 1930s, the French inventor Charles Mochet's Velocar (**1**) smashed the world mile and kilometre records, but the international cycle racing body banned such machines. Modern interest dates from the founding of the International Human-Powered Vehicle Association (IHPVA) at Long Beach, California in 1976. By 1980, a two-man version of the

1

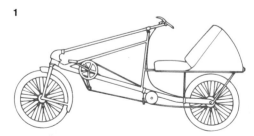

2

3

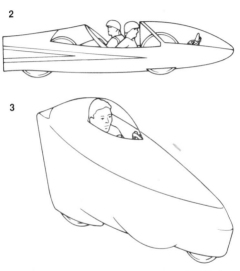

Vector (**2**) had won the 200m flying start at 101.3kph (62.9mph), more than 30km (18.6mi) faster than the fastest conventional bicycle. In 1986, Fred Markham covered 200m at 105.4kph (65.5mph) in the Easy Racer Gold Rush (**3**). In England, in 1990, Pat Kinch powered the Bean (**4**; overleaf), covering 75.6km (47mi) in an hour, beating the official record by nearly 50 per cent. The Bean has front-wheel drive (**a**), smooth tyres (**b**)

and a sleek fibreglass shell (**c**), producing only about one-third of the drag of an ordinary racing bike and rider.

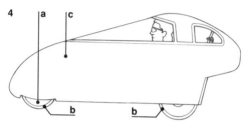

STREET RECUMBENTS

The racing triumphs of streamlined recumbent bicycles and tricycles have inspired small-scale manufacturers to design machines for everyday use. Some are ready-made, others come as kits, with or without a streamlined fairing to boost speed and protect the rider from the weather. Advantages over ordinary bikes include fast cruising speeds for less effort, more powerful brakes and reduced risk of getting hurt if you capsize (there is less far to fall). Disadvantages include high cost, increased weight, crosswind risks to fully faired machines, and a low profile which reduces the rider's visibility and makes the vehicle difficult to see in traffic. (Flying a conspicuous pennant from a mast helps to solve that problem.)

Here we show examples of two types of design. The Windcheetah SL (**1**) is a long-wheelbase recumbent trike with frame (**a**), pedals (**b**), transmission (**c**), steering (**d**) and seat (**e**) arranged or designed as in no ordinary tricycle.

The Kingcycle (**2**) is a short-wheelbase recumbent bicycle with hydraulic brakes (**a**) and a flexible backrest (**b**) supported by the front of a luggage container (**c**). Short-wheelbase recumbents are faster than ordinary bikes and more agile than long-wheelbase machines.

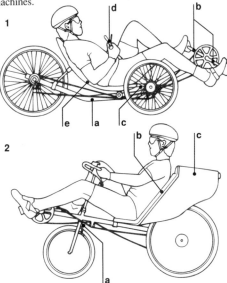

PEDALLED AEROPLANES

Cyclists can even power lightweight, glider-like
aeroplanes. In 1977, cyclist Bryan Allen pedalled the
screw-driven Gossamer Condor (**1**) in a figure of eight
around a half-mile (0.8km) course near Shafter,
California. Created by designer Paul MacCready, the
fragile aircraft with its rear-mounted propeller (**a**) had a
29.3m (96ft) wingspan, yet weighed only 31.8kg (70lb)
thanks to its cardboard, balsawood and aluminium
tubing, wire struts and plastic skin.

In 1979, pedalling at 75 revolutions per minute, Bryan
Allen flew MacCready's 28.7m (94ft) wingspan
Gossamer Albatross (**2**) 35km (22mi) across the
English Channel at an airspeed of 13.7kph (8.5mph).
Headwinds made this exhausting feat equal to flying
56km (35mi) in still air.

1

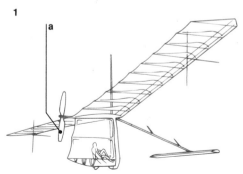

In 1988, Kanellos Kanellopoulos pedalled the Daedalus (**3**) 119km (74mi) from Crete across the Aegean Sea to Thíra at nearly 30kph (about 18.5mph). This amazing feat celebrated the Greek legend of Daedalus, an inventor whose wings supposedly bore him from Crete to Sicily. The 34.1m (112ft) wingspan Daedalus was a Massachusetts Institute of Technology project. Pedalled aeroplanes are hard to propel and easily upset by strong winds. For everyday use, the best human-powered machine will always be a bike.

2

3

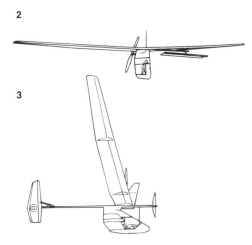

PEDALLED BOATS

Pedalling a small, screw-driven craft can be faster than
rowing a similar boat, because oars waste energy and
set up wind resistance. In the 1890s, three cyclists in a
screw-driven boat (**1**), pedalled 162.5km (101mi) down
the Thames from Oxford to Putney in under 19 hours. It
took 1 hour longer for three university oarsmen to row
the same distance.

Pedal power was banned from racing, but by the 1980s,
the International Human-Powered Vehicle Association
revived interest in such machines. New designs for
waterborne HPVs appeared. By the early 1990s, the
fastest HPV craft was a pedal-driven hydrofoil (**2**),
which reached 29.8kph (18.5 mph) over 100m (328ft).

1

2

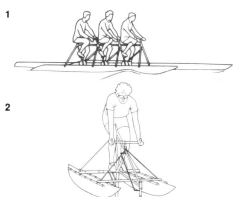

Index

COLLINS GEM

Other Gem titles that may interest you include:

Gem Atlas of Europe
A fully up-to-date atlas of the new Europe,
including plans of 37 major European cities   **£3.50**

Gem First Aid
Describes all major first aid procedures with clear
illustrations   **£3.50**

Gem Holiday Games
A varied selection of indoor and outdoor games to
play on holiday   **£3.50**

Gem Card Games
A handy guide to the rules and strategies of play for
a wide variety of popular family card games   **£3.50**

Gem SAS Survival Guide
Includes camp craft, first aid, navigating and
surviving in different climates and terrain   **£3.99**

Gem Castles of Scotland
A pocket-sized guide to 100 of Scotland's most
dramatic castles and strongholds   **£3.50**

COLLINS GEM

Bestselling Collins Gem titles include:

Gem English Dictionary (£3.50)
Gem Calorie Counter (£2.99)
Gem Thesaurus (£2.99)
Gem French Dictionary (£3.50)
Gem German Dictionary (£3.50)
Gem Basic Facts Mathematics (£2.99)
Gem Birds (£3.50)
Gem Babies' Names (£3.50)
Gem World Atlas (£3.50)